CLASSIC
TRACTORS

Publications International, Ltd.

Manufactured in China.

8 7 6 5 4 3 2 1

ISBN 13: 978-1-4127-1223-1
ISBN 10: 1-4127-1223-8

Library of Congress Control Number: 2005903626

Acknowledgments

The editors would like to gratefully acknowledge the cooperation of the following contributors and owners who made this book possible:

The Danbury Mint; M.B.I., Inc.
ERTL/Racing Champions
Ford Motor Company Archives
The Franklin Mint
McCormick-IHC Archives - State Historical Society of Wisconsin
Ray Heller, Case Archives

Tractor Owners

Antique Gas & Steam Engine Museum, John Bauer, Howard Bonner, H.G. Bouris, Patrick Desjardins, Allen Dilg, John Dilg, Kenneth Dutenhoeffer, Lee Dyal, Pete Dykstra, Alan Fredrickson, Sam Hutchinson, Bruce Johnson, Ralph L. Johnson, Don Klingen, Ron Luse, Charlene Meyer, Robert Meyer, W.C. Milligan, Jon H. Peterson, Jim Schneiter, Julius & Gary Schnell, Ted Segerstrom, Scott & Sheryl Stier, Ray Volk, Al Wagner, Gary Wagner, Tom Walther, Lew Weaver.

Photography by Vince Manocchi and Doug Mitchel.

Thanks also to Wayne and Scott Rosenberger for sharing their invaluable knowledge.

CONTENTS

FOREWORD

What we now call "tractors" began to appear in the late 1800s, but they were hardly recognizable as such. Steam powered and looking like slightly scaled-down locomotives, they were complicated beasts of mammoth proportions and great expense. After the turn of the century, gasoline-powered tractors appeared that were smaller and cheaper, making them more accessible to the average farmer.

Early tractors typically carried two horsepower ratings: the first being at the drawbar (pulling power), the second at the belt pulley (used to drive equipment). Power at the drawbar would always be less due to frictional losses in the driveline, and the figures would be expressed in numbers such as "12-25." Tractors might also be rated by how many plows could be pulled, such as a "three plow" machine. When the power take-off (PTO) became almost universal after World War II, the trend was to list only PTO horsepower (very close to pulley horsepower), which is how tractor ratings are expressed today.

In the colorful history of tractors, a few events stand out. The first was the 1917 debut of Henry Ford's Fordson, its low price bringing mechanization to more farmers. The second was a 1919 Nebraska law requiring any tractor sold in the state to pass rigorous testing, and since the results were publicized, it served to weed out many substandard machines. The third was the introduction of pneumatic rubber tires in the late Twenties, which replaced steel wheels and were proven to transfer more power to the ground—and fewer bumps to the backside. A Thirties innovation was the three-point hitch, which kept the plow digging at a consistent depth and prevented the tractor from flipping over on itself if the plow struck an obstacle. "Styled" tractors appeared about the same time, displaying both cosmetic advances and improved ergonomics. Arriving after World War II was hydraulic operation of towed implements, which added time-saving convenience.

Although this book focuses on the glorious tractors that brought mechanization to the nation's farms, let us not forget the hardy souls for whom they were built. A good tractor guided by the able hands of a hard-working farmer is a century-old partnership that has helped to feed our nation—and the world.

1895
Russell Steam Tractor

Like their automotive counterparts, early tractors were powered by steam as often as internal combustion. And the Russell brothers of Massillon, Ohio, were well-versed in the science of steam.

C.M. Russell & Company was founded around 1840 by Charles, Nahun, and Clement Russell, who were all trained as carpenters. The brothers began experimenting with steam engines in the late 1870s, eventually turning them into their primary vocation.

Though steam shovels appeared earlier, the company's first steam-powered tractor arrived in 1887 producing a rousing six horsepower. By the time our featured example was built in 1895, horsepower had risen to 30 at the pulley. That still might not sound like much, but steam engines were well-suited to heavy hauling, and pulling this ten-ton beast through a dirt field—to say nothing of pulling a plow—was heavy hauling indeed.

Creature comforts were few in those days, and standing behind a steam boiler in the heat of summer surely taxed the hardiest souls. The example pictured sports a canopy roof, which was likely a mixed blessing; though it kept the sun out, it also kept the boiler heat in.

As Otto-cycle engines became more efficient and gasoline more plentiful, Russell & Co. added gas-powered tractors to the line in 1909. But although its machines were respected for their ruggedness, the company fell victim to a competitive marketplace and folded in 1927.

1902
Advance Steam Tractor

L ike many early tractor manufacturers, Advance
Thresher Co. started out making farm implements.
Incorporated in 1881, it was building a 12-horsepower
steam tractor by the late 1890s, those machines being
very similar in appearance to the 1902 model shown here.
And speaking of similar appearances, note how much the
Advance resembles the earlier Russell—and how much
both look a bit like a steam locomotive.

Like the Russell, the Advance used a single-
cylinder engine mounted above the boiler. The machine
carried an 8-16 rating, which meant it produced 8 horsepower at the drawbar (indicating how much power was
available to pull an implement), 16 at the pulley (which
was used to drive other machinery; it's shown on the
opposite page just above the rear wheel). The difference
between the two ratings is due to frictional losses in the
driveline, which decreased in later years with the advent
of better lubricants, more-efficient gears, and lower-
friction bearings.

Steam tractors of the day were not only heavy, cum-
bersome, and complicated, they also were inefficient
and often required as much as two hours to build up a
head of steam. Nonetheless, they survived for several
years after internal-combustion engines came into
common use.

1913
Case Steam Tractor

Jerome Increase Case incorporated J.I. Case & Company in 1863 after 20 years of developing and selling threshers and other implements in Racine, Wisconsin. The company began producing portable steam engines to power treadmills and rotary sweeps in 1869, followed some years later by a steam traction engine, which was self-powered but required horses to steer it.

A steering device was added to the traction engine in 1886, forming the basis for the company's first tractors. Some of those steam traction engines were huge: a 150-horsepower version built between 1905 and 1907 weighed a whopping 18 tons. Though gas-engined models joined the line in 1911,

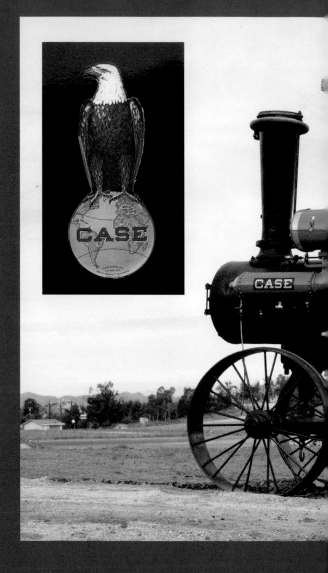

1913 Case Steam Tractor

steam-powered tractors continued in production until 1924.

The 1913 Case steam tractor shown here produced 40 horsepower at the pulley from an 8.25-inch bore and 10-inch stroke. It's apparent that many steam tractors of the period followed a rather consistent design philosophy, bearing more than a casual resemblance to steam locomotives.

1917
Best 60

D aniel Best started building steam traction engines in the late 1880s, continuing until he sold out to a competitor, The Holt Manufacturing Company, in 1908. But two years later, Daniel's son formed C.L. Best Gas Traction Engine Company, putting Best and Holt in competition once again.

Though it started out with wheeled tractors, Best was building crawlers by 1913. The first was a big 75-horsepower model, followed by a host of smaller versions from 18 to 60 horsepower, as well as a larger 90-horse model. Best's engines carried four individually cast cylinders sporting overhead valves—an unusual configuration for the day, but oddly enough, the same as many of Holt's. Both companies fitted large plates to the

Continued on page 21

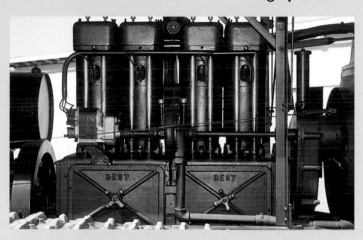

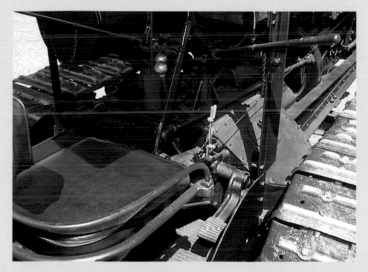

1917 Best 60

sides of the crankcases to allow easy access to the bearings. Also like Holt, Best's early crawlers often had front wheels for steering.

The manner in which power was transferred to the tracks differed somewhat, however. Best used a differential that allowed both tracks to be powered in a turn for better pulling power, but that meant the machine couldn't turn very sharply. Holt powered each track individually. Power was cut off to the inside track in a turn, which enabled it to execute tighter turns but diminished pulling power in the process. Both turned with the aid of track brakes.

Though hardly the biggest crawler in the company's lineup, the Best 60 nonetheless tipped the scales at a portly 17,000 pounds plus. Later testing revealed that the 1128-cubic-inch engine produced "only" 56 horsepower, a bit less than its rating.

Competition between the two manufacturers raged until 1925, when they merged once again to form Caterpillar Tractor Company. Certain models from both lines continued in production, but Caterpillar's real claim to fame was its 1931 introduction of the country's first diesel-powered tractor.

21

1917
Holt 75

After first building wagons and then combines, Benjamin Holt produced his first commercially viable steam-powered crawler in 1904. With their tracks providing a long, wide "footprint," these vehicles could be used in soft soil that wouldn't support the weight of a traditional wheeled tractor or even a horse. Gasoline-powered versions appeared in 1908. Though some wheeled vehicles were produced along the way, The Holt Manufacturing Company has always

23

been known for its crawlers.

Early Holt crawlers typically had one or two wheels mounted in front of the tracks for steering (what we'd now call a "halftrack"), while later models abandoned the wheels in favor of cutting power to the inside track and applying a track brake. Sizes ranged from a relatively small 18-horsepower model to a six-cylinder 120-horsepower behemoth.

The 75 pictured here carries a 1414-cubic-inch four-cylinder engine producing (as the name implies) 75 horsepower. It's no lightweight, tipping the scales at nearly 12 tons.

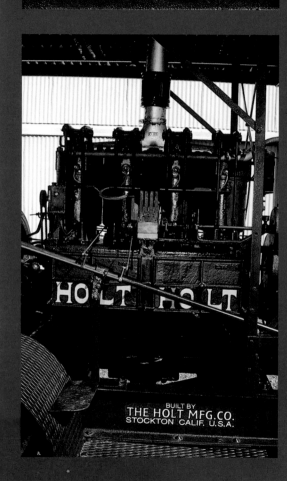

BUILT BY
THE HOLT MFG.CO.
STOCKTON CALIF. U.S.A.

1918
Holt Caterpillar 45

It was during field testing of an early model in 1904 that Holt's friend Charles Clements remarked that the movement of the track reminded him of a caterpillar. Holt picked up on the name, which would later be applied to all the company's products—and eventually, to a company itself.

While early Holt crawlers relied on one or two wheels mounted in front of the tracks for steering, later versions steered by cutting power to and then braking the inside track.

The 30-horsepower "Baby Caterpillar" of 1914 was one of the first Holts to do without front steering wheels. Our featured Caterpillar is of similar design but is larger and carries a 45-horsepower rating. Most Holt engines of the period were large-

No 20371

CATERPILLAR

27

No 20871

28

displacement four-bangers, unusual in that they had individually cast cylinders with overhead valves.

Holt's biggest competitor of the time was the C.L. Best Gas Traction Engine Company, makers of Best crawlers. The two companies merged in 1925 to create the Caterpillar Tractor Company—a name inspired by the comment made during a field test more than 20 years earlier.

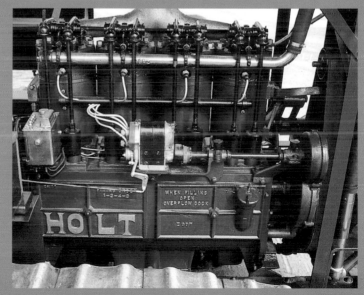

1918
International Harvester
Titan 10-20

International Harvester Company grew out of the merger of McCormick and Deering, both renowned manufacturers of grain harvesters—and for many years, cutthroat competitors.

McCormick was originally formed by Cyrus Hall McCormick, who gained fame—and no small fortune—as the inventor of the reaper. This machine appeared on the market in the early 1840s, adding a binder in the 1870s.

William Deering began his career in the dry goods business, but he joined with a partner to sell Marsh Harvesters

TITAN
MFD BY
INTERNATIONAL HARVESTER COMPANY
CHICAGO, U.S.A.

in 1873. Deering took over the business upon his partner's death and started selling a binder of his own in 1880.

By the turn of the century, McCormick and Deering had twice attempted a merger—and twice failed. But terms were finally agreed upon in 1902 that gave birth to the agricultural giant known as International Harvester.

International began work on gas engines shortly after the merger, and its first tractors hit the fields in 1906. Growth was rapid; within five years, the company was leading the industry in sales.

Oddly, International's equipment was initially sold under two slightly different names. McCormick dealers carried an IH Mogul line, while Deering dealers sold IH Titans. The machines were later sold with either McCormick-Deering or International nameplates, the former eventually fading away.

Single-cylinder models appeared first, followed shortly by opposed twins. Like most competitors of the era, these early machines were quite large—and expensive. But the marketplace was calling for smaller, cheaper tractors, and International obliged.

The two-cylinder Titan 10-20 arrived in 1915, selling a phenomenal 78,000 copies through 1922. These machines were renowned for their power, dependability, and ease of service, and were among the few small tractors to sell well against Ford's low-cost Fordson.

1920
Minneapolis 35-70

L ike so many other early tractor manufacturers, Minneapolis Threshing Machine Company (MTM) started out making farm implements. Organized in 1887, MTM built and sold threshing machines, but soon added steam traction engines from Huber Manufacturing Company to its product line.

MTM began making its own steam traction engines in 1891. But by 1911, it was evident that gasoline engines were the wave of the future,

1920 Minneapolis 35-70

and the company began selling a 20-horsepower gasoline tractor made by Universal Tractor Company. It was not an exclusive contract, however; the same unit was sold under several different brand names, one being the Rumely GasPull.

At about the same time, MTM contracted with Walter J. McVicker to design a tractor it could call its own. It was initially built for MTM by Northwest Thresher Company, sales commencing in late 1911, but MTM was soon building tractors itself. Over the years, these covered a range from 15-30 horsepower to 40-80, though these were rerated in 1920 at 12-25

1920 Minneapolis 35-70

and 35-70, respectively. The largest examples, one of which is shown here, were quite sizable indeed; at left it's seen dwarfing a 1927 Fordson tractor.

The 35-70 was powered by a 1486-cubic-inch four-cylinder engine that was mounted transversely across the frame. The huge "sideways" radiator contributed to a 50-gallon coolant capacity. Though simpler in operation than the old steam-powered tractors, there was still plenty to keep the driver busy.

Combines joined the MTM line in 1925. Four years later, MTM was merged with Minneapolis Steel and Machinery Company (another tractor manufacturer) and Moline Plow Company to form Minneapolis-Moline Company, which would later become one of the largest implement and tractor manufacturers in the United States.

1921/1927
Fordson

After the runaway success of his Model T, Henry Ford applied a similar formula to a tractor for the masses. But despite his considerable resources, the project did not go altogether smoothly.

First, there was the question of the name. "Ford," of course, would have been the obvious choice, but it was already taken. A company in South Dakota had hired a man named Ford, ostensibly a tractor engineer (which he wasn't), so it could rightfully use his name on its tractors; an obvious—though legal—way to capitalize on Henry Ford's reputation. The original Ford Tractor Company went into receivership in 1916, but the name was then transferred to another company in

1921/1927 Fordson

Minnesota—owned by the same individual. Relatively few of these Ford tractors were built, reportedly due to poor quality.

Henry countered by forming the Ford Tractor Company in 1917 and using the name "Fordson" on his machines. Being small, light, and inexpensive, they immediately shot to the head of the sales race—despite reviews that were not altogether favorable.

As with the Model T before it, Henry dropped the Fordson's price over the years, prompting competitors to do the same. This brought the cost of tractors down to where more farmers could afford one.

The Fordson eventually was upstaged to the point that even a low price couldn't sell it, and it was dropped in 1928—though production continued in Europe. However, Ford would reenter the U.S. tractor market a decade later with a larger model boasting significant improvements.

Above: A Fordson is shown during field tests before going on sale in late 1917. Henry Ford (center) was raised on a farm, and thus knew firsthand the rigors of the trade. Right: A Fordson ad from the mid Twenties stresses the advantages of a tractor to farmers still using horses.

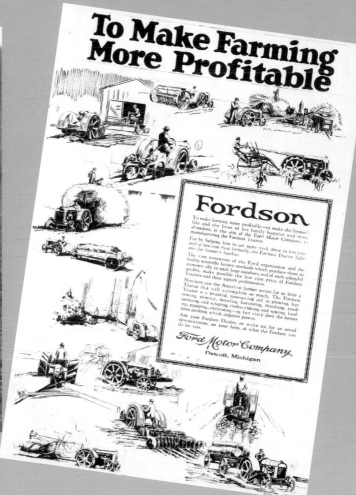

1921/1927 Fordson

Above: A threshing machine is driven off the pulley of a Fordson via a long leather belt. Early tractors were as often used for powering equipment as for pulling plows. Right: A Fordson fitted with crawler tracks and wooden skis hauls an impressive load of logs through the snow.

1921/1927 Fordson

Above: A 1925 Fordson display shows off both the tractors and the implements they could pull. Right: Crowds turn out to see the wares of a Fordson dealer in early 1926. Even at that time, horses were still the primary source of power on most small farms.

1921
Samson Model M

After introducing its first tractor in the mid Teens, Samson was purchased by General Motors Corporation in 1917. No doubt the General's intent was to field an instant competitor to the Fordson built by crosstown rival Ford Motor Company.

Sold under the slogan "The Strength of Samson in Every Part," early models were fairly light (for a tractor) and built low to the ground for good stability on sidehills. However, these machines not only looked crude compared to the Fordson but were more expensive as well, and the design was abandoned in 1919 when Samson introduced the Model M.

Samson Model M

The Model M looked similar to a Fordson but was slightly heavier and more powerful. None of this was by accident. At 3300 pounds it weighed 600 pounds more than the Ford, and its four-cylinder engine displaced 276 cubic inches versus Fordson's 251, producing 11.5 drawbar horsepower versus 9.3. It even "happened" to be offered in the same red-on-grey color scheme.

Despite its apparent advantages, the Samson was short-lived. Competition from Henry's Fordson spelled the end for many tractor manufacturers, and Samson was one of them. Shortly after producing our featured Model M in 1921, GM decided to abandon the tractor business and leave the farming to Ford.

1921 Samson Model M

Samson Model M

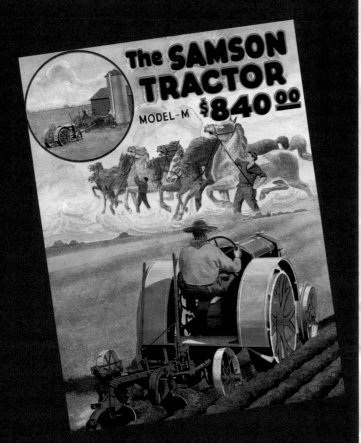

A Samson sales brochure from the early Twenties promotes the tractor's features and advantages. At $840, it cost more than twice as much as a Ford Model T car.

SAMSON

Burns gasoline or kerosene without change or adjustment. Tank holds 22 gallons with large hand-holes —reserve tank 3 gallons

Air cleaner keeps motor clean of dirt and dust

Large radiator allowing ample cooling space, tubular type large hand-holes for easy cleaning and filling

MODEL M TRACTOR $840

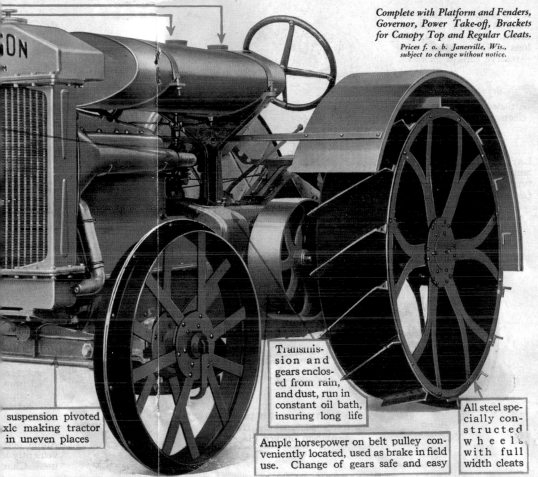

Complete with Platform and Fenders, Governor, Power Take-off, Brackets for Canopy Top and Regular Cleats.

Prices f. o. b. Janesville, Wis., subject to change without notice.

suspension pivoted xle making tractor in uneven places

Transmission and gears enclosed from rain, and dust, run in constant oil bath, insuring long life

Ample horsepower on belt pulley conveniently located, used as brake in field use. Change of gears safe and easy

All steel specially constructed wheels with full width cleats

1922
Fordson F Crawler

Within mere months of its introduction in late 1917, Ford's little Fordson had became the best-selling tractor in the land. Though much of its early success was sparked by the need for higher food production during World War I, sales continued to climb after the Armistice. The reason was simple: Just like its Model T cousin, the Fordson's remarkably low price made it affordable to the masses.

It did have limitations, however. Being among the smallest and lightest tractors built, Fordsons weren't made for bigger jobs. As the demand for greater pulling power increased, sales were lost to larger machines, and this competition brought the Fordson's price down even further: from around $700 at introduction to just $395 by 1922.

Yet, what it lacked in capability it made up for in flexibility. Due to its

1922 Fordson F Crawler

low initial cost and vast numbers, Fordsons were adapted to all sorts of different tasks. As with the Model T, aftermarket equipment abounded, and inventive owners often built their own. One such modification replaced the wheels on each side with huge, rotating pontoons sporting spiral "tracks" that essentially converted the tractor into a snowmobile—albeit a very slow one.

More common was a crawler conversion. So equipped, a Fordson combined light weight and a large footprint to yield great traction along with minimal ground pressure—perfect for use in sandy or soggy soil. This example is fitted with a Trackson Model F crawler conversion. As with most other tracked vehicles, turning was accomplished by slowing down the inside track.

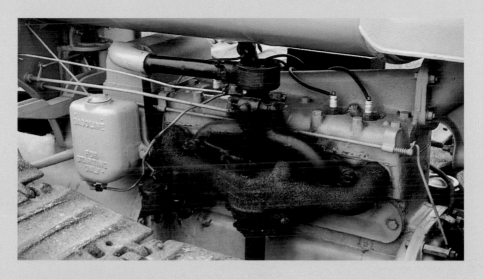

1922 Fordson F Crawler

1926
McCormick-Deering
15-30

In an effort to combat the inexpensive Fordson that had allowed Ford Motor Company to surpass International Harvester in sales, IH introduced the famous 15-30 in 1921. Badged a McCormick-Deering (the two major companies that merged in 1902 to form IH), it was the first of the company's tractors to use unit construction: a one-piece cast-iron "frame" running from front to rear that formed the engine crankcase, transmis-

McCORMICK-DEERING

sion case, and differential case. This design saved weight and simplified assembly. It also resulted in cleaner styling, which was aided further by a vented engine cover.

As with many others of the period, the four-cylinder engine could be run on either gasoline or kerosene. Though a traditional belt-drive pulley was

1926
McCormick-Deering 15-30

fitted to the right side, newly optional was a rear-mounted PTO (Power Take-Off). Note the rubber tire treads that have been bolted to the steel wheels; these were often added when the machine was to be driven on paved roads.

Though the Fordson held a substantial price advantage, the 15-30 proved extremely popular. Nearly 100,000 copies were sold through 1929, at which time a revised version with a slightly larger engine, promoted as the "New 15-30 Tractor," carried on until 1934.

1926
Rumely OilPull M20-35

R umely became a well-known and respected
tractor manufacturer after introducing its
first such machine in 1910. Previously, Rumely
had built threshers and steam engines, but an
agreement with John Secor, who had been
experimenting with fuel-burning engines, produced the first OilPull tractor. Within nine
months, more than 100 were built.

By 1913, Rumely had purchased Gaar Scott &
Company, Advance Thresher Company,
American Abell, and the Northwest Thresher

1926 Rumely OilPull M20-35

Company, all competitors. But Rumely was hit hard the following year by a poor crop that left numerous buyers unable to make payments on purchased tractors, and the company went into receivership. It was reorganized as Advance-Rumely Thresher Company in 1915.

Early OilPulls were powered by huge single- and twin-cylinder engines of up to 1885 cubic inches and 75 horsepower. Though called the 30-60, Rumely underrated that model, as it did with all its machines. Smaller tractors arrived later, including the M20-35 model featured here. Like other OilPulls, it carried a large chimney-shaped radiator in front, and the 601-cubic-inch engine was cooled by oil, not water.

Another round of financial problems struck Rumely during the Depression, and the company was purchased by Allis-Chalmers in 1931.

Case 12-20

L ike many early manufacturers that started with steam-powered tractors, Case adopted gasoline engines as technology made them more practical. The first of these appeared in 1911, and like its steam-powered predecessors, it was huge. But the move was to smaller tractors, made possible by the relative compactness of a gasoline engine, and Case was quick to follow this trend as well.

Case's early gas models used four-cylinder engines mounted crosswise in the frame. This configuration was

Continued on page 81

felt to deliver a greater percentage of available power to the drawbar, since the engine was rotating in the same direction as the wheels; a differential that had to "turn" the power 90 degrees was less efficient.

Introduced in late 1921, the Case 12-20 looked to be all engine. A cast-iron crankcase made up the main frame section, and the extremely short wheelbase contributed to a very stubby appearance— and a very tight turning radius. Spoke wheels were replaced by cast steel wheels, which were lighter and less expensive.

Compared to the Fordson, the 12-20 was heavier (about 4200 pounds total) and its 267-cubic-inch overhead-valve engine produced more power. While far more expensive than the Ford, many felt it was money well spent.

The 12-20 was renamed the Model A in 1928 and then disappeared. After that, Case abandoned cross-mounted engines for more-conventional longitudinal mounting.

1927 Case 12-20

BETTER
FARMING
WITH
BETTER
TRACTORS

Showing Simplicity of

FAN SHAFT MOUNTED ON
ANTI-FRICTION
BEARINGS

DUST-PROOF
MAGNETO

4 CYLINDER HEAVY DUTY
CASE ENGINE 4½×6

BRAKE FOR
PULLEY

BELT
ON
FC

STEEL AXLE
AUTOMOBILE TYPE

IMPULSE MAGNETO
COUPLING

CAST FRAME
TUBULAR
RADIATOR

DUST-PROOF
HUBS

SPEED
GOVERNOR

ENCLOSED SPIRAL
GEAR FAN DRIVE

SHAFT
ON BALE

SHING   CUT STEEL DROP FORGED   ENCLOSED   ENCLOSED DROP FORGED
                    PINION   CUT SPUR GEAR   MACHINED AND HARDENED
                                                          STEERING GEAR

TED   SEMI-STEEL
                                 CUT SPUR GEAR   ROLLER BEARINGS

                                                    SHAFT MOUNTED
                                                   ON ROLLER BEARINGS

                                                              ONE PIECE MAIN
                                                                  FRAME

                                                              SWINGING
                                                              DRAW BAR

                                                          DUST-PROOF GEAR
                                                              HOUSING

                                                          ENCLOSED SPUR
                                                          GEAR FINAL DRIVE

ING CRANKSHAFT   CUT STEEL DROP   CUT STEEL FORGED,
TH MAIN BEARINGS   FORGED, HARDENED   HARDENED, ONE PIECE
    INCHES   BULL PINION   MASTER GEAR
         CUT STEEL DROP FORGED   ROLLER
HARDENED TRANSMISSION GEARS   BEARINGS

A Case sales brochure from the early Twenties included a cutaway drawing of the tractor's unusual powertrain arrangement. Most tractors of the day had their engines mounted longitudinally, parallel to the wheels. Case claimed that mounting its four-cylinder engine crosswise allowed more of its power to reach the rear wheels—which was probably true.

83

1928
Caterpillar 60

Caterpillar Tractor Company was formed in 1925 with the merger of competitors C.L. Best Gas Traction Engine Company and The Holt Manufacturing Company. Best and Holt were both known for their crawler tractors, so it was a logical union. Holt held the "Caterpillar" trademark, which it had been using as a model name for many years, and after the merger, models from both compa-

1928 Caterpillar 60

ny's product lines continued under the Caterpillar brand.

Weighing in at a "svelte" 10 tons, the Sixty was powered by a huge four-cylinder gasoline engine of 1128 cubic inches. During this period, it was the largest Caterpillar offered; smallest was the Ten, which weighed a little over two tons, with a number of others in between.

In 1928, the purchase of the Russell Grader Company put Caterpillar in the road-grader business, and three years later it introduced a diesel-powered crawler, the first of its kind. Since then, the company has expanded into earth-moving and construction equipment, for which it is best known today.

1929
John Deere GP

John Deere, perhaps the most recognized name in farming equipment, got its start as Deere & Company in 1837, when its founder built his first steel plow from an old saw blade. Other implements and machines followed, either by invention or acquisition of other companies, but it wasn't until 1918 that Deere offered its first tractor.

Having already spent substantial sums and countless hours on experimental tractors with little to show for its efforts, Deere purchased the Waterloo Gasoline Engine

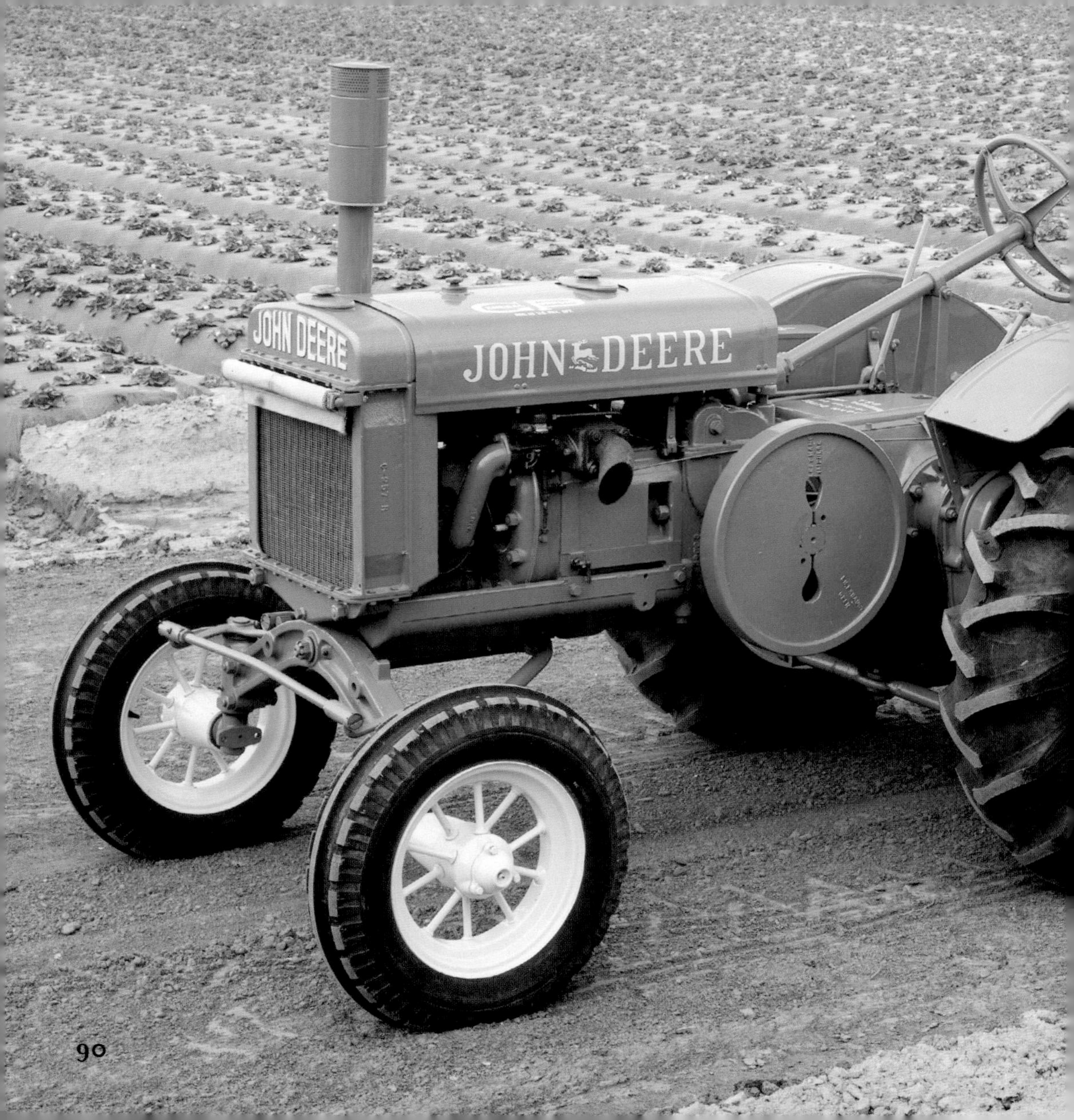
JOHN DEERE
JOHN DEERE

Company—and was in the tractor business overnight. The Waterloo Boy Model N was a 12-25 rated machine with stout construction and a sterling reputation. Today it has the distinction of being the first tractor run through the Nebraska Tests, which were initiated in March 1920.

Close on the heels of the Waterloo Boy came a tractor based on Deere's own experiments: the Dain All-Wheel Drive. Named after Joseph Dain, lead engineer on the project, it had three wheels (two front, one rear, all driven) and was also rated at 12-25, but was somewhat smaller than the N. Though blessed with modern styling and great traction, only 100 were built between 1918-1919, after which production ceased.

Out of Waterloo's experimental department came the venerable 15-27 Model D in 1923. Much smaller, lighter, and more modern than the previous Model N, it was an instant success, and would remain in the Deere line—with numerous improvements, of course—for a phenomenal 30 years.

Finally came the Model GP (General Purpose) featured here. Smaller than the D with a 10-20 rating, it was introduced in 1928 and was soon offered with narrow or wide front track. It became the first John Deere to offer a power equipment lift. Early models were fitted with traditional steel treads; the pneumatic tires on this example were added later.

1929
Twin City 21-32

In 1929, three compa-
nies merged to form
Minneapolis-Moline
Company: Moline Plow
Company, Minneapolis
Threshing Machine
Company, and
Minneapolis Steel and
Machinery Company.
Among Minneapolis-
Moline's first products
were Twin City tractors
carried over from the
Minneapolis Steel and
Machinery line.

One such tractor was
the 21-32, which was
introduced around the
time of the merger. It
was powered by a 382-
cubic-inch four-cylin-
der overhead-valve

engine with full-pressure lubrication, working through a three-speed transmission. It weighed about 6300 pounds.

This particular example is still owned by the same family that purchased it way back in 1929. It worked bean fields until being retired in 1947, and then essentially sat idle until receiving a well-deserved restoration in 1990.

1930
Hart-Parr 18-36

Hart-Parr's rich history in the tractor business began in 1897, when University of Wisconsin engineering students Charles W. Hart and Charles H. Parr designed a gasoline engine.

Moving to Iowa in 1900, the partners built their first tractor the following year. After instituting a number of improvements, the fledgling company produced fifteen of its 17-30 rated tractors in 1903. The 17-30's two-cylinder engine displaced 2042 cubic inches; safe to say, it was not a high revver. Neither were the company's single-cylinder engines that came along in the mid to late Teens—despite displacing a "mere" 785 cubic inches.

Like most other tractors of the day, early Hart-Parr machines were quite large, typically weighing in at 7 to 10 tons. But they were among the few to be driven by gas engines rather than steam, and were cooled by oil rather than water. The largest appeared in 1911 as the 60-100, a huge beast with 9-foot rear wheels and a 26-ton curb weight.

By the late Teens, the company had phased out its heavy oil-cooled models to concentrate on smaller tractors that were then in vogue. These were powered by similarly smaller horizontally mounted two-cylinder engines providing rated power of 10-20 to 18-36, though later

1930 Hart-Parr 18-36

four-cylinder models (made by placing a pair of two-cylinder engines side-by-side) carried ratings up to 28-50.

The 18-36 pictured is among the last tractors built to the design of the original Hart-Parr firm. Its two-cylinder engine displaced 501 cubic inches—a far cry from the monstrous engines of old—and drove through a three-speed transmission.

In 1929, Hart-Parr merged with three other companies to form the Oliver Farm Equipment Company (later, simply Oliver Corporation). Though some of the corporations' early tractors were called "Oliver-Hart-Parr," they were powered by new inline vertical four-cylinder engines.

1930

Massey-Harris was formed in 1891 with the merger of Massey Manufacturing Company and A. Harris, Son & Company, both of Canada. Like many other mergers, it was a joining of staunch competitors; in this case, Canada's number-one and number-two implement manufacturers.

Another purchase, that of J.I. Case Plow Works in 1928, put M-H solidly in the tractor business. The Plow Works is not to be confused with J.I. Case Threshing Machine Company, which also made tractors—and which quickly purchased sole use of the "J.I. Case" name from M-H.

1930 Massey-Harris 4WD General Purpose 15-22

The Plow Works had been marketing Wallis tractors, which were unique in their use of a boiler-plate frame—often recognized as the first step toward unit construction—which did away with separate frame rails. These tractors were considered some of the best of their day, and soon wore the Massey-Harris name.

But another tractor offered by M-H didn't follow the Wallis design. The General

Purpose was a 15-22 rated four-wheel-drive model powered by a Hercules four-cylinder engine of 226 cubic inches. High-mounted front and rear differentials drove the wheels through large reduction gears.

Despite its apparent advantages in low-traction conditions, the 4WD 15-22 didn't sell well and was discontinued by 1937.

1936
John Deere BW

In 1934, Deere brought out the Model A, which slotted between the D and GP in size and power. The A introduced adjustable wheel tread to the tractor field, and by the time the model was discontinued in 1952, would rate among Deere's best-selling tractors of all time.

Closely following the A was the little Model B of 1935. Often referred to as "two-thirds of an A," it closely resembled its bigger brother. The B was the smallest tractor in the John Deere line, just slightly trailing the GP—which it

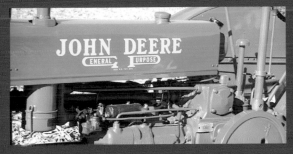

soon replaced. Rated at 9-14, it was offered in numerous configurations: single- and dual-front-wheel tricycles; regular and wide front tread in regular or high clearance; and orchard and industrial models. The "W" in our featured BW indicates it has the wide front axle. Bs carried the one-piece transmission casting originating on the A, along with central-mounted hitch and power take-off. Also like the A, they enjoyed a long life—though not quite as popular of one.

Even in the early Thirties, it has been estimated that only one in five farms used a tractor; it was the Depression, and gas power still wasn't an economical replacement for horse power on farms under 100 acres. But the low-priced B went a long way in helping to mechanize these smaller farms, often being the first tractor to till their fertile lands.

1936 John Deere BW

1937
Allis-Chalmers WC

A llis-Chalmers started out a little differently than
most early tractor manufacturers, which typically
grew out of farm implement businesses. In 1861, Edward
Allis purchased a firm making equipment for flour mills,
renaming it Edward P. Allis & Company. Allis soon
became interested in steam engines, and had his first one
in operation by 1869. At the turn of the century the company was the largest producer of steam engines in the
country.

In 1901, Allis merged with Fraser & Chalmers, a
machinery and stamping mill, to form Allis-Chalmers.
Numerous other companies were added in future years,
but the corporate name remained the same.

1937 Allis-Chalmers WC

It wasn't until 1914 that the company produced its first tractors, but this end of the business grew quickly and became its own division in 1926. Following that was a series of acquisitions, most notably the 1931 purchase of Advance-Rumely Thresher Company, maker of the Rumely OilPull tractor.

Early Allis-Chalmers tractors appeared in a variety of configurations, including three-wheeled and front-drive versions. By 1919, more conventional machines were being produced, and in 1929, Allis-Chalmers became one of the first manufacturers to offer pneumatic tires on its tractors as an option—albeit, an expensive one. About this time, corporate colors changed from green to orange.

Introduced in 1934, the WC was powered by a 201-cubic-inch overhead-valve four-cylinder engine providing 28 horsepower at the pulley on gasoline, 24 on distillate. It remained in "unstyled" form until 1939, when it was fitted with new sheetmetal, including a grille to cover the previously exposed radiator.

While early Case models were famous for their cross-mounted four-cylinder engines, the company switched to longitudinal mounting in the late Twenties, when row-crop tricycle models also appeared.

The first of Case's row-croppers was the CC, represented by the 1937 model shown here. Save for the front-end design, it was nearly identical to the com-

CASE

pany's model C, which carried a traditional wide-track front. Adjustable rear wheels accommodated various row widths, and a power take-off was optional. The CC carried an overhead-valve 259-cubic-inch four-cylinder engine delivering 22 horsepower at the drawbar, 29 at the pulley on kerosene.

Early Case row-croppers used an unusual steering system. A large cast piece resembling the frame and yoke of a bicycle was simply bolted to the front of the radiator support, with the steering arm jutting out the left side. A long tie rod extended from the arm back to the steering box located at the rear of the hood. One advantage was that farmers could later switch over to a traditional front end if so desired. This rather awkward-looking setup continued even after Case introduced "styled" tractors in the mid Thirties.

1937
International Harvester
Fairway 12

Introduced late in 1934, the Fairway 12 was originally sold as a McCormick-Deering model. The 1937 version seen here is virtually identical, except that it wears International Harvester's corporate badging.

As the machine's name suggests, the Fairway was marketed as a golf-course tractor designed to be at once gentle and tough. It could pull up to nine mowers, as well as handle general course-improvement work. The 12's 113-cubic-inch four-cylinder engine developed 18.9 horsepower.

1937 International Harvester Fairway 12

Pumps, compost mixers, and other machines could be operated off the optional belt pulley or the standard power take-off.

At 110 inches, the 12's turning radius was tight—ideal for close work at the edges of fairways or near hazards—and allowed close cutting around shrubbery. Wide wheels (8 inches in front, 16 inches at the rear) and a relatively light weight of 3000 pounds combined to produce a gentle footprint. The smooth-faced wheels lacked the traction lugs fitted to farm tractors—for obvious reasons.

Despite being well-suited for its specialized duty, the Fairway's life span was brief. Production ended in 1938 after just 600 were built.

Largest of Allis-Chalmers' machines of the Thirties was the Model A, introduced in 1936. Power came from a 461-cubic-inch four-cylinder engine charged with moving the tractor's 7100 pounds. Fourth gear allowed a road speed of up to 10 mph.

Rated to pull four plows, the A's brutish demeanor was never hidden behind the cloak of stylish sheetmetal, as it remained "unstyled" through the end of its

production run in 1941. All told, only about 1200 were built, making it quite rare—even in its own time.

Part of the A's limited appeal was no doubt due to a rather high price: At $1495, it cost nearly three times as much as Allis-Chalmers' own Model B. It was simply more tractor than most farmers of the era needed...or at least, could afford.

1938
Allis-Chalmers B

Allis-Chalmers' smallest tractor of the Thirties also proved to be its most popular. From its introduction in 1937 to the final edition 20 years later, more than 127,000 were produced.

The Model B carried a 116-cubic-inch four-cylinder engine good for 10 horsepower at the drawbar, over 15 at the pulley. Its high stance and adjustable tread width (from 40 to 52 inches) made it perfectly suited to cultivating, which was still done by hand or with draft animals on many small farms of the era. A simple design kept weight to under 2700 pounds and the price to just $518 by 1940.

Part of the B's legacy is that it was the first Allis-Chalmers tractor to be "styled." Though perhaps not as svelte as some others of the period, it maintained a modern, purposeful look, and its general contours would set the pattern for many of the company's machines to come.

1938
Allis-Chalmers Motor Patrol

A horse of a different color—or at least, a different design—was this Allis-Chalmers Motor Patrol. Based on the WC model introduced in 1934, it featured an extended frame that allowed a large road-grader blade to be mounted at an angle between the front and rear axles. Though intended for use on farms for both road grading and terracing (cutting ledges into the sides of slopes to slow water run-off), few farmers could justify the

1938 Allis-Chalmers Motor Patrol

high cost for such a specialized machine. This one, like many others, was originally purchased by a municipality for use in leveling dirt roads.

Like the WC, the Motor Patrol was powered by a 201-cubic-inch overhead-valve four-cylinder engine. Running on gasoline, it produced 28 horsepower at the pulley; on cheaper distillate fuel, it produced 24. The two large wheels to the operator's left and right raised and lowered the blade, which was also adjustable for angle and could be moved side to side.

1938
John Deere BNH

Deere's entry-level B line came in a multitude of versions sporting different front axle designs and ride heights, each tailored to different uses. Model designations reflected this and were quite self-explanatory once you knew the lingo; for instance, the BNH designation of our featured tractor stands

for a Model B with Narrow front axle and High clearance—admittedly a little redundant, as the narrow front axle dictated a high clearance.

However, there are two types of "narrow" fronts. One is as seen here: a single front wheel held "bicycle style." The other mounts two wheels close together on an axle that tilts them so that they nearly touch at the bottom. Either can be found on what are termed "tricycle" tractors, but the two-wheeled versions are far more common. In both cases, the idea was that the front wheel drove between two crop rows, while the rear track could be adjusted to straddle the same two rows (different crops are planted in different row widths). These are often referred to as "row crop" tractors because of that design intent.

By 1938, pneumatic (rubber) tires were becoming more popular as their prices came down. Tests indicate a given tractor could pull more weight on pneumatic tires than on steel wheels—and be more economical and comfortable to boot.

1938
John Deere D

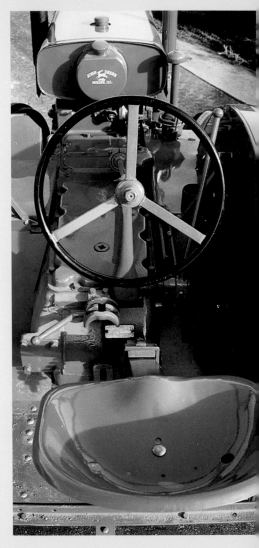

Deere's largest tractor during the Thirties was the Model D, introduced in 1923. It replaced the Model N, which was a huge, old-fashioned tractor originating as the Waterloo Boy. The Model D has the distinction of being the first new tractor born under the John Deere name, though its design origins dated back to Waterloo.

When Deere purchased Waterloo in 1918, it had no idea the longtime tractor manufacturer had anything new up its sleeve. The company's Waterloo Boy, later renamed the John Deere Model N, was a large, sturdy tractor of considerable reputation—and had been for some time. It wasn't until the buyout went through that someone introduced Deere's executives to Waterloo's experimental department.

What surfaced was a modern tractor so advanced and well thought out that it would directly influence John Deere's designs for the next 40 years.

Continuing from the Model N was a horizontally mounted two-cylinder overhead-valve engine laid crosswise in the frame, with the cylinders pointing forward. Some competitors at the time were touting four-cylinder engines, but Waterloo's engineers were convinced that two cylinders were sufficient for tractor applications while being cheaper to build and maintain.

When introduced to the market in 1923, the Model D's engine displaced 465 cubic inches, resulting in a 15-27 rating. A bore increase in 1927 brought displacement up to 501 cubic inches. Early versions had a six-spoke flywheel that doubled as the crank starter; by 1926, this was changed to a solid flywheel for safety reasons. The steering wheel, originally mounted on the left side of the tractor, moved to the right side in 1931.

The 1938 example shown represents the last Model D to be offered only in "unstyled" form. Though the model designation would carry on for another 15 years, the tractor it graced would present a decidedly different face to the world.

1938 John Deere D

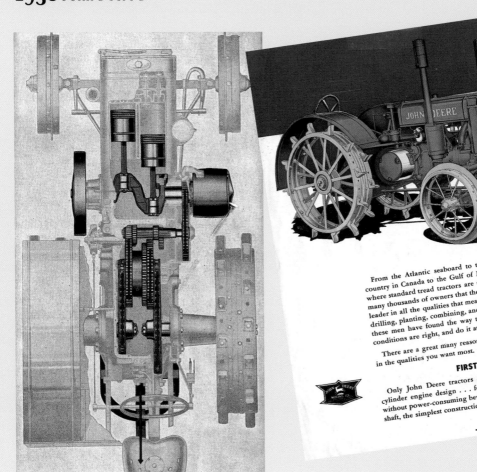

THE
Leade

From the Atlantic seaboard to the west coast, from the P...
country in Canada to the Gulf of Mexico, and in all parts of
where standard tread tractors are used, it is the universal opi...
many thousands of owners that the John Deere Model "D" Tr...
leader in all the qualities that mean greater farm profit. Plow...
drilling, planting, combining, and threshing—in all kinds of ...
these men have found the way to save time, get their work...
conditions are right, and do it at rock-bottom cost.

There are a great many reasons why the John Deere Mod...
in the qualities you want most.

FIRST IN SIMPLICITY

Only John Deere tractors give you the simplicity of
cylinder engine design . . . fewer parts . . . a straight-li...
without power-consuming bevel gears . . . a belt pulley ri...
shaft, the simplest construction possible.

- 2 -

in all the QUALITIES
that mean GREATER Farm Profit

FIRST IN DEPENDABILITY

Only John Deere two-cylinder tractors give you the dependability of fewer and sturdier parts ... greater ability to stand up under heavy loads ... proper distribution of weight for better, more positive traction.

FIRST IN ECONOMY

Only John Deere two-cylinder tractors are backed by a long-time record of success, efficiency and safety in burning the low-cost fuels such as distillate, furnace oil, fuel oil, stove tops, Turner Valley naphtha, and some grades of Diesel oil ... fuels that cost far less and are approximately 10% more powerful ... fuels that the John Deere converts into steady, dependable power on drawbar and belt. Burning the low-cost, money-saving fuels in a John Deere tractor is *no experiment.*

But fuel economy is not all. John Deere Model "D" owners also benefit from another great economy ... the ability to inspect and adjust their tractors right on the farm. The simplicity of two-cylinder design makes possible complete accessibility, one of the big reasons

why a recent survey shows that 82% of John Deere owners do fully 75% of their own service work.

EXTRA-LONG LIFE

To the other great features listed, add the extra years of service that the John Deere Model "D" gives, to better understand the big swing to John Deere two-cylinder power. Fewer, heavier, longer-lived parts ... the use of high-quality materials, careful workmanship, and rigid inspection ... make records of 8, 10, and even 12 or more years of service not at all unusual.

Low-pressure rubber tires are available for the John Deere Model "D" Tractor when specified.

- 3 -

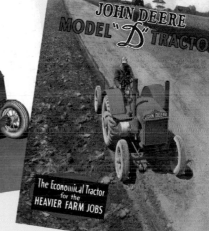

With their "flat" two-cylinder engines, John Deere claimed its tractors were easier to work on compared to four-cylinder competitors, a strong selling point when the nearest service facility could be miles away. This sales brochure for the Model D waxes poetic over the tractor's virtues.

1938
John Deere L

When John Deere introduced the little Model L in 1938, it was aimed at farmers still using horses for plowing and cultivating. Being a one-plow-rated tractor, it could replace a two-horse team. But its small size and low price (about $465 at introduction) also made it popular for grooming lawns at golf courses and estates.

The Model L differed from its larger stablemates in several respects. Frames consisted of two steel tubes that were attached in front to a large cast member underneath the grille, and the front axle was set back further than in other Deere designs.

Also, the L ventured from the usual Deere power-train arrangement. The engine was a small 57-cubic-inch Hercules-built vertical twin mounted longitudinally in the frame, and it was mated to a three-speed manual transmission from a Ford Model A car. Cost was the overriding reason for using outside suppliers for these parts, but familiarity with the automotive-

style shifter and clutch for
first-time tractor owners
was another consideration.

One "big tractor" feature
of the little Deere was its
independent rear brakes,
which worked in conjunc-
tion with the differential to
allow tighter turns. Two
separate brake pedals (one
for the left brake, one for
the right) could be operated
independently or together
with the right foot.

147

1939
Ford 9N

After setting the tractor industry on its ear with the 1917 introduction of the Fordson, Ford dropped out of the market in 1928. Though the tractors had sold in vast quantities in the early years after their release, sales dwindled as the machine's limitations became known, and dropping the price to bolster volume during the Depression also cut profits. By the late Twenties, competition had once again become fierce, and Ford pulled up stakes.

During World War I, an Irishman named Harry Ferguson had developed a new type of tractor hitch that improved plowing efficiency. He had approached Henry Ford with his idea, but Ford evidently was not impressed. However, Ferguson continued to refine the design to incorporate even more benefits, the result being the famous Three-Point Hitch. In 1938, Ferguson met with Ford again, and this time Henry saw the light.

Ford incorporated Ferguson's hitch in its new 9N tractor introduced the following

year. Called the "Ford Tractor with Ferguson System," it again made waves in the industry. Slightly larger than the Fordson, the 9N featured a 120-cubic-inch flathead four-cylinder engine rated at 12.6 drawbar horsepower and 23 at the belt—not much more than the final Fordsons. But updated technology and the Ferguson system made the difference; that and a $595 price that included rubber tires, electric starter, power take-off, and the Three-Point Hitch. It was an instant hit.

Due to limited capacity at the stamping plant, some of the first 9Ns came with cast aluminum hoods. Our featured example is one of them. Though the aluminum hoods were originally painted the same color as the rest of the tractor, this one has been polished for effect.

1939
Massey-Harris 101

Massey-Harris introduced "styled" tractors in 1938, and they were stylish indeed. Radiators were hidden behind curved grilles, engines were concealed with louvered panels, and all the edges were rounded off. Furthermore, Massey's colors were changed from green with yellow trim and red wheels (similar to John Deere and nearly identical to Oliver) to red with yellow accents.

Though earlier M-H tractors used engines built in-house, most of those manufactured after the styled models were introduced carried engines built

by outside suppliers—primarily Continental and Chrysler. The 101 pictured here is powered by a flathead six-cylinder Chrysler of 201-cubic-inch displacement. It provided 24 drawbar horsepower and 36 at the belt. The "Twin Power" designation comes from the fact that peak drawbar horsepower was achieved at 1500 rpm, while maximum pulley horsepower came at 1800 rpm.

An interesting comparison between steel wheels and pneumatic rubber tires, both of which were offered—and tested—on this model, reveals the substantial differences between the two. Steel-wheeled versions weighed significantly less (3805 pounds on steel, 5725 on rubber), but also delivered less power at the drawbar (18 horsepower versus 24). Many tractors of the period offered both, but rubber tires were a rather expensive option, sometimes doubling the initial cost. However, the payback occurred not only in greater pulling power, but also in better fuel economy and a far more comfortable ride.

MASSEY-HARRIS

1939
Minneapolis-Moline
UDLX Comfortractor

Minneapolis-Moline was formed in 1929 through the merger of Minneapolis Threshing Machine Company, Minneapolis Steel and Machinery Company, and the Moline Plow Company. The company's first products were Twin City tractors carried over from the Minneapolis Steel line, but eventually the company's products wore Minneapolis-Moline badges. Though

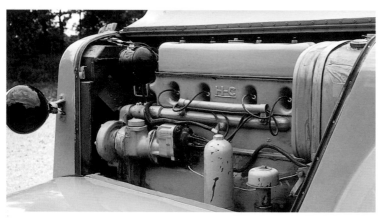

1939 Minneapolis-Moline UDLX Comfortractor

stoutly constructed and some-times innovative, the company's tractors were fairly conventional in terms of styling. Except, that is, for the UDLX Comfortractor.

Radical for its time, the UDLX was the first tractor to sport an enclosed cab, and along with its "styled" hood and fend-ers, looked like a cross between a car and a tractor. And that's exactly how M-M promoted it: as a hard-working farm machine that could be driven to church on Sunday. Unfortunately, it only managed to sell that idea to about 125 buyers—and even that took three years.

Of course, the price didn't help; at $1900, the UDLX cost as much as a conventional trac-tor *plus* a Pontiac eight-cylinder sedan. But its 283-cubic-inch four-cylinder engine combined with a five-speed transmission to

allow road speeds up to 40 mph, and luxuries such as radio, heater/defroster, and windshield wipers were available. Passengers entered through a door at the rear of the cab, which boasted carlike appointments.

Today, of course, cabs are common on tractors, proving the UDLX was just too far ahead of its time.

1941
International Harvester Farmall AV

International enjoyed enormous success with its Farmall A tractor, which was introduced in 1939. It was versatile and tough, yet easy on fuel and sufficiently compact to be ideal for smaller farms. In its initial iteration, the A ran with a 113-cubic-inch four-cylinder engine producing 16.3 horsepower at the drawbar, 18.3 at the pulley. An operator's position that was high relative to the engine cowl gave unusually good visibility, making the A well-suited for crops that could be easily damaged. A popular variant of the A, seen here, was the high-riding AV, which offered a full half-foot more ground clearance than the A. A large selection of attachments, to be installed at the factory or in the field, was available to AV owners. Front and rear wheels were offered in a variety of heights. Belt pulley and power take-off were optional. In 1940, a base AV sold for $660. Production of the A ceased in 1947, when it was superseded by the Super A.

1941
John Deere B

By the late 1930s, John Deere tractors had received styling makeovers by industrial designer Henry Dreyfuss. However, for the first few years, most model lines contained both "styled" and "unstyled" versions selling side by side.

Deere's Model A and B were the first to get the treatment in 1938. Radiators were encased behind sheetmetal grilles, while the forward-mounted steering mechanism was concealed behind a strong vertical spine.

Hoods that were once simple engine covers were graced with "extruded" lines. Spoked wheels began to give way to solid wheels. Not all the improvements came at once, however; it wasn't until later, for instance, that the square-section frame rails were replaced by graceful pressed-steel rails.

And it wasn't just appearances that were altered. Part of the redesign philosophy was to ease the operator's job as well, so comfort of the seat (which was finally padded) and driving position were improved, along with the placement and operation of controls.

Model B engines of the era displaced approximately 175 cubic inches, yielding about 16 horsepower on the drawbar and nearly 20 at the pulley. Running through a six-speed transmission, top speed was around 12 mph.

Though Deere's larger Model A held greater popularity during the period, the Model B sold more than a quarter-million copies during its 13-year production run. It was finally put out to pasture in 1952, along with its Model A sibling.

1944
John Deere Lindeman

Jesse Lindeman began selling crawler tractors in 1922; first Holts, later Cletracs. He was based in Washington state, where fruit trees were commonly planted in the sandy soil. Eventually Lindeman became a John Deere dealer, and sometime in the early 1930s he mated an old set of Best tracks to Deere's biggest tractor, a Model D. The steering wheel was replaced by a pair of control sticks that activated track brakes on each side, and while this arrangement didn't work as well as track clutches, it was sufficient for the purpose. Customers liked what they saw, and what started out as an experiment turned into a business.

Lindeman switched to smaller Deere Model GP tractors after they became available and then added track clutches to enhance turning capabilities. Adaptations for the Model B followed, one of which is shown here. While the "John Deere" name retained top billing, "Lindeman" was cast into the track side-plates.

1944 John Deere Lindeman

Deere itself had built some prototype crawlers at about the same time Lindeman started up, but they never went to market. In 1946, Deere asked Lindeman to help with development of a crawler version of the upcoming Model M, and Lindeman did more than help; he sold Deere his company.

1945
Ford 2N

Supplies of many materials became scarce during World War II, metal and rubber among them. So in order to conserve these resources, Ford modified its 9N tractor to use less of both.

Though the new 2N looked very similar to its predecessor, an electric starter and generator were no longer standard, engines reverting to hand cranks. Likewise, pneumatic tires, which had become almost universal on new tractors by the early Forties,

were traded for antiquated steel rims. Some pieces were lightened by making them out of tubular steel rather than solid beams.

Like most of these later tractors that were built with steel rims, the 2N pictured has since been fitted with rubber tires. But it has also been fitted with a different engine.

Oliver Glover was a Ford tractor dealer who attained a patent on a kit to exchange the 2N's stock 120-cubic-inch flathead four-cylinder for Ford's automotive 226-cubic-inch flathead six. But the conversion wasn't as simple as it might sound.

Because the 2N was of unit construction, with the engine, transmission, and differential forming the "frame," the front axle originally was bolted directly to the engine's beefy cast-iron oil pan. But the automotive engine used a flimsy stamped-steel oil pan, so the front end had to be bolted to special frame rails. Also, an extension was added to the rear of the hood, which was mounted farther forward to clear the larger engine. All in all, however, it was a fairly inexpensive way to nearly double the power output, and it's estimated that around 10,000 were built.

1945
International Harvester Farmall M

Interational Harvester's Farmall M is
the most recognizable and arguably the
most enduring of all IH wheeled tractors. To many, its mix of grace and hardy
aggressiveness sums up not just IH, but
the American tractor experience in
general.

The M was introduced in 1939, the
year that also saw the debut of its A-, B-,
and H-series stablemates. All four were
row-crop tractors designed to perform
basic, everyday cultivation. Between 1939
and the end of production in 1952, IH
produced just under 280,000 Farmall

M tractors, as well as some 8300 high-clearance models and other special variants.

Farmall Ms tested in 1939 at the Nebraska Test Laboratory summoned about 39 belt horsepower and 24 drawbar horsepower from a 248-cubic-inch overhead-valve four-cylinder engine, enough to be considered three-plow machines. By 1940, the Farmall M could be ordered with a swinging drawbar, electric starter and lights, and Lift-All hydraulic system, along with earthmovers and a vast selection of other special attachments. So popular was the M series that it was joined in 1950 by a modified "Super" series, some of which were available with diesel engines. Another variant, the 1948-51 Farmall C, utilized a frame similar to that of the H and M series.

1946
John Deere D

For many years, Deere's Model D was the workhorse of the lineup—and looked it. Short and stocky compared to its siblings, the D offered a styled version in 1939 that made it appear even more so. Radiators were covered with a chunky vertical-bar grille, the hood added contour lines, and fenders took on a smoother appearance.

Since its debut in 1923, the D carried John Deere's biggest horizontal twin, mounted crosswise in the frame in what would become a company tradition. That engine grew somewhat for 1927,

from 465 to 501 cubic inches, thanks to a bore increase. It remained that size through the end of D production in 1953, when it was rated at 30.8 horsepower at the drawbar, 38.2 at the pulley.

When fitted with rubber tires, those tires were huge, looking like donuts compared to other models' hula hoops. They contributed substantially to the D's near-5300-pound heft. The Model D continued to use a three-speed transmission when most competitors had four speeds, though that didn't seem to hurt its popularity; the D's 30-year production span was the longest of any Deere in the company's lengthy history.

1946
John Deere LA

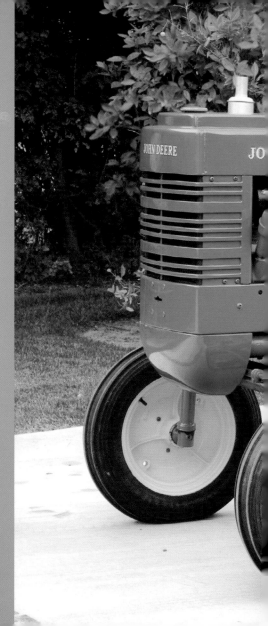

When introduced in 1938, Deere's little Model L was powered by a longitudinally mounted 57-cubic-inch vertical twin built by Hercules. Its intent was to mechanize small farms still using horses, but it also found use for light hauling duties on larger farms as well as lawn mowing.

That first year, the L was "unstyled," with exposed radiator and running gear capped by a simple sheetmetal hood. A styled version appeared for 1939 boasting fancy grillework, sculpted hood, and enclosed driveline. But unlike the larger Deere models, which carried both unstyled and styled versions of the tractors concurrently in the line, the unstyled L was dropped when the styled version appeared.

In 1941, the L was fitted with a larger, Deere-built version of the Hercules vertical twin, and the designation was changed to LA. This engine displaced 66 cubic inches and could be fitted with a

generator and electric starter. It produced half again as much horsepower as the original Hercules unit: 7 at the drawbar, 10.4 at the belt pulley. Overall weight of the tractor didn't change much, the LA tipping the scales at just over 1500 pounds.

This 1946 model represents the last of the breed. The L and LA had served their purposes well, but the larger, more conventional-looking Model H, introduced in 1939, would carry on as Deere's smallest offering.

JOHN DEERE
MODEL LA TRACTOR

EVERY DAY
Check oil level in engine.
Remove dirt from Air Cleaner cup
and put in new oil (SAE-30).

ONCE A WEEK
Grease 18 Alemite Fittings.
(Use gun grease).

EVERY TWO WEEKS,
or at end of 60 hours operation. Drain
and refill crankcase in engine—Use
SAE-30 oil in summer, use SAE-10W oil
in cold weather—crankcase holds three
quarts.
Oil Fan Bearing—(Same oil as in
engine).
Check oil level in following:
Clutch Shaft Housing
Transmission   —(SAE-90 Oil)
Final Drives

TWICE A YEAR
Pack front wheel bearings with grease.
Drain and refill with oil to plug level:
Clutch Shaft Housing
Transmission and Differential
Final Drives
Fill Steering Gear Housing to top.
(Use SAE-140 Oil)

TIRES
Front—28 lbs. air pressure
Rear—12 lbs. air pressure

1946
Oliver OC-3

James Oliver made his mark with the invention of the chilled plow in 1855. What made this such a monumental advancement—and gave it the "chilled" label—was that the cast iron was sprayed with water during the cooling process, which annealed the surface so that it was smoother and harder without being brittle.

Oliver's company was called the South Bend Iron Works. In 1929, it merged with tractor-maker Hart-Parr and implement manufacturers Nichols & Shepard and American Seeding Machine to form Oliver Farm Equipment Company.

At that time, Hart-Parr's large twin-cylinder tractors gave way to smaller four-cylinder machines originally labeled "Oliver-Hart-Parr."

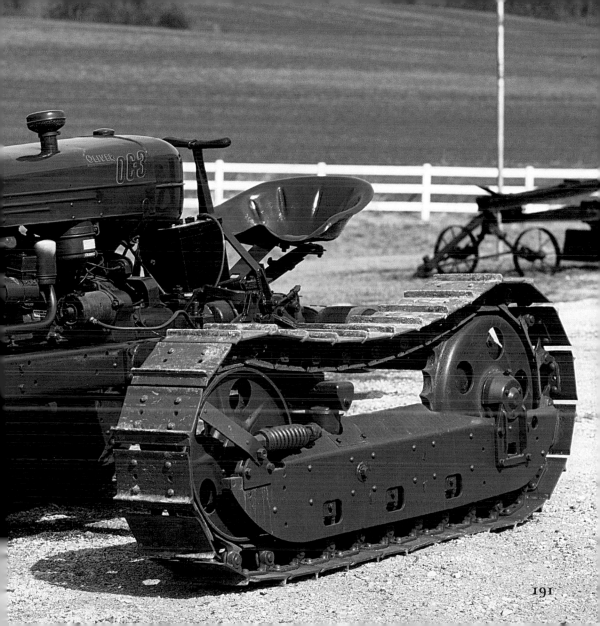

1946 Oliver OC-3

Fairly conventional in appearance, they were followed in the mid Thirties by streamlined six-cylinder models with louvered bodywork enclosing the engine—quite radical for the time—though some unstyled four-cylinder tractors remained in the line. At that point, "Hart-Parr" was dropped from the badge, leaving only the "Oliver" name.

Though known mostly for its smooth-sided tractors with rounded, laid-back grilles, Oliver did produce some crawlers as well, as witnessed by this OC-3 of 1946. Several sizes of OC crawlers were offered, all offshoots of Cletrac models built by Cleveland Tractor Company, which Oliver purchased in 1944. This OC-3 is powered by a 132-cubic-inch Hercules four-cylinder engine delivering 21 horsepower at the drawbar.

1947
International Harvester
Orchard O-4

Because fruit bruises easily or can be inadvertently knocked from branches altogether, it was imperative to orchard and grove owners that they have a low tractor designed for plowing, disking, and furrowing among fruit trees. Hence International's O series, which stood just 57 inches high, and carried exhaust systems and air cleaners that mounted flush with the tractor sides rather than sticking up over the hood as in other models. Like its somewhat more hardy companion, the O-6, the O-4 labored in citrus groves and orchards where branches were low and trees closely spaced. (The OS-4, OS-6, and ODS-6—a diesel—were for use in areas where trees were more widely separated and pruned fairly high.)

The O-4 seen here lacks the standard streamlined fender cowlings and optional steering wheel cowl that presented smooth surfaces to the trees, ensuring that branches or fruit would not be snagged. The fender covers were

removable, and in such a configuration the O-4 was well-suited for work in vineyards.

The O-4 could handle a two-plow setup, while the larger "6" tractors could manage a three-plow attachment. Primary fuel for the O-4 was gasoline, but it also ran effectively on cheaper and lower-grade distillate fuel.

The four-cylinder engine had pressure lubrication; replaceable cylinders; and precision, quick-replaceable main and connecting rod bearings. Maximum belt horsepower with gasoline was 27.5; with distillate, 24. Max drawbar horsepower with gasoline was 25, while distillate gave a drawbar rating of 22. A 5-speed transmission allowed very slow first-gear travel for spraying, and rapid fifth-gear travel that topped out at 14 mph. A hand-operated over-center clutch allowed the operator to clutch or declutch while sitting or standing.

1947 International Harvester Orchard O-4

1948
Case LA

Case's Model L, introduced in 1929, was the first of the company's tractors to use a longitudinally mounted engine; previous examples had the engine mounted "sideways." It was Case's largest offering of the period, and also one of the first tractors of any make to use pressure lubrication.

An update of the L appeared in 1941 as the Model LA. Built from 1940 to

Continued on page 204

1948 Case LA

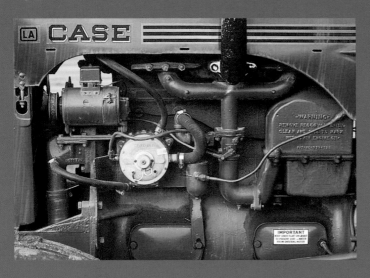

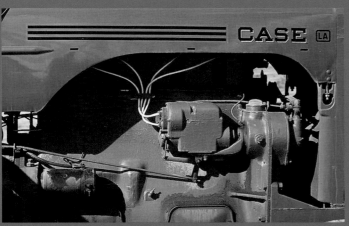

203

1952, it carried on as the company's flagship, but incorporated a number of improvements.

Like the L, power came from a 403-cubic-inch four-cylinder engine, but the LA offered versions that could run on tractor fuel, gasoline, or LP Gas. Each allowed progressively higher compression ratios, which resulted in increasing levels of power: Tractor fuel yielded 46.6 horsepower; gasoline 55.6, and LP Gas, like the model shown, 57.9 (notice the round pressure tank mounted in front of the steering wheel, and the silver pressure regulator on the left side of the engine). A "road gear" increased top speed from 5.5 to 10 mph.

Unlike the original L, the LA was a "styled" model, though not to the degree of many competitors. A curved, sheet-metal grille covered the radiator, but the LA maintained a chunky, business-like appearance.

Case's VA series came out in 1942 to replace the similar V series, which was only two years old at the time. Both were smaller tractors rated for one or two plows, but the V used a 124-cubic-inch Continental flathead four-cylinder engine, while the VA had a Case-built overhead-valve four of the same size. The VA produced 17 horsepower on tractor fuel, 20 on gasoline, and was available with either a high- or low-mounted exhaust system. Standard equipment included a four-speed transmission allowing a top speed of 10 mph, individual differential brakes for tighter turns, and an electric starter.

During its life cycle, a variety of styles was offered,

1948 Case VAO

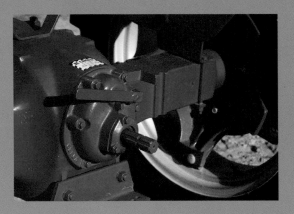

including standard front track (VA), row-crop tricycles (VAC), high clearance (VAH), and orchard style (VAO). Both front and rear tracks were adjustable for width except on tricycle models, which were the first row-crop tractors to be offered by Case. The VAO orchard version, shown here without the full bodywork that included wheel enclosures, side shields, and cowl attachments, was built lower to the ground than other models for added clearance under tree limbs.

Unlike its V-series predecessor, the VA led a fairly long life, even by tractor standards. It carried on until 1955, after which it was replaced by the more powerful 300 series.

209

1948
International Harvester
Farmall H

Although the Farmall H was officially introduced in 1939, seven units left the IH factory in 1938 under a Model 2-F designation. The H, a rugged and versatile tractor, was related to the Farmall A, B, and M models, and remained in production until 1953, when the run concluded with a few Super H models. Early H tractors were available with steel wheels, rubber tires, or a steel-rubber split. During World War II, tight controls on the production and sales of rubber hurt farmers as well as

drivers of automobiles, and the Farmall H was thus slow to make the transition to all-rubber tires.

The H, like some other IH tractors, could use gasoline or lower-grade distillate to power its 152-cubic-inch four-cylinder engine, which was rated at nearly 24 horsepower at the pulley, 20 at the drawbar on gasoline. A special variant, the Farmall HV, was a high-clearance row-crop machine.

The 1948 H on these pages farmed in Sterling, Illinois, until the late 1960s. It subsequently sat in a field for more than 25 years before its restoration during the first half of 1999.

1948
John Deere A

John Deere's Model A was introduced in 1934, just as the nation's economy was beginning to rebuild after the Great Depression. Times were still tough, however, and the vast majority of farms continued to use horses in the fields.

A number of innovations first saw the light of day on the A. It was the first Deere to mount the power take-off (PTO) and hitch along the tractor's centerline, which allowed an attached implement to be pulled straight. Rear track widths were adjustable, and differential brakes allowed the inside wheel to be slowed for tighter turning. Hydraulics made their debut, easing the strain of lifting implements by hand at the end of the rows. A 309-cubic-inch horizontal twin provided 23 pulley horsepower

1948 John Deere A

and 16 at the drawbar, enough to pull two plows.

When first introduced, the A came as a two-front-wheel tricycle. Soon afterward, single front wheel, regular front track, adjustable wide track, and high-clearance models were offered. In 1939, "styled" Model As appeared (though unstyled versions continued in the line), along with a larger 321-cubic-inch engine with 20 drawbar and 29 pulley horsepower.

When the A was finally retired in 1953, it held the distinction of being Deere's most popular tractor—and still is today.

1948 John Deere A

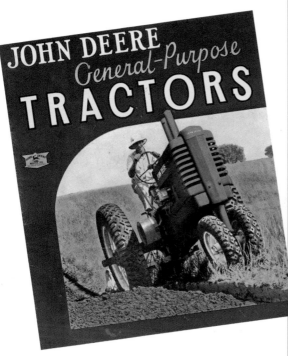

A late-Thirties sales brochure for the Model A and B features a cutaway drawing that reveals John Deere's famous flat-twin engine. It also shows Deere's vertical, front-mounted steering gear, which ran "naked" on unstyled models, but was concealed by a sheetmetal cover on styled versions (above).

COMFORTABLE. Large, bucket-type seat rides on a spring-mounted, channel-steel support. Roomy platform enables operator to sit or stand at will.

EASY TO OPERATE controls—clutch, thrott shift, etc. — are withi reach of the operator fr tractor seat.

PROPER LINE OF DRAFT. Swinging drawbar is permanently located. Has a wide range of adjustment.

EFFICIENT POWER TA Furnished as standar ment on John Deere purpose tractors. a bath of oil.

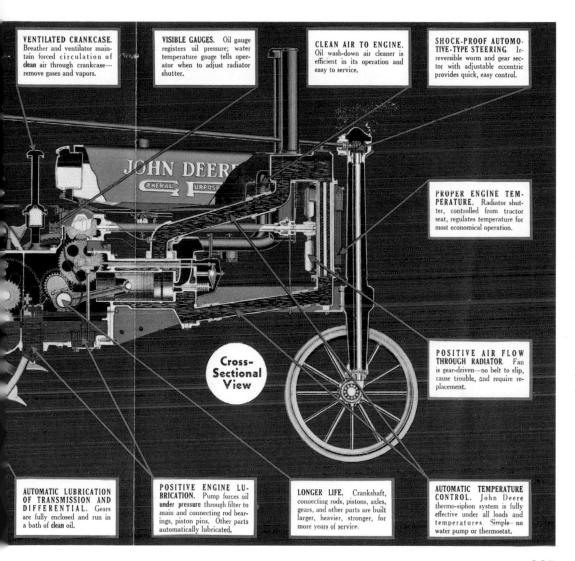

VENTILATED CRANKCASE. Breather and ventilator maintain forced circulation of clean air through crankcase—remove gases and vapors.

VISIBLE GAUGES. Oil gauge registers oil pressure; water temperature gauge tells operator when to adjust radiator shutter.

CLEAN AIR TO ENGINE. Oil wash-down air cleaner is efficient in its operation and easy to service.

SHOCK-PROOF AUTOMOTIVE-TYPE STEERING. Irreversible worm and gear sector with adjustable eccentric provides quick, easy control.

PROPER ENGINE TEMPERATURE. Radiator shutter, controlled from tractor seat, regulates temperature for most economical operation.

POSITIVE AIR FLOW THROUGH RADIATOR. Fan is gear-driven—no belt to slip, cause trouble, and require replacement.

JOHN DEERE

GENERAL PURPOSE

Cross-Sectional View

AUTOMATIC LUBRICATION OF TRANSMISSION AND DIFFERENTIAL. Gears are fully enclosed and run in a bath of clean oil.

POSITIVE ENGINE LUBRICATION. Pump forces oil under pressure through filter to main and connecting rod bearings, piston pins. Other parts automatically lubricated,

LONGER LIFE. Crankshaft, connecting rods, pistons, axles, gears, and other parts are built larger, heavier, stronger, for more years of service.

AUTOMATIC TEMPERATURE CONTROL. John Deere thermo-siphon system is fully effective under all loads and temperatures Simple—no water pump or thermostat.

A very popular tractor of the Forties and early Fifties was the Case DC, a row-crop tricycle model in the company's D series, which was its second largest of the period next to the LA. Production of the Model Ds ran from 1939 to 1955.

Though boasting "styled" sheetmetal, the DC retained the prominent (some might say awkward-looking) external steering gear originating on the CC model of the Thirties. Other D-series models included the standard-tread D, the high-crop DH, and the DO orchard version, all of which had lower-mounted, less-obvious steering systems to go with their standard-tread front ends.

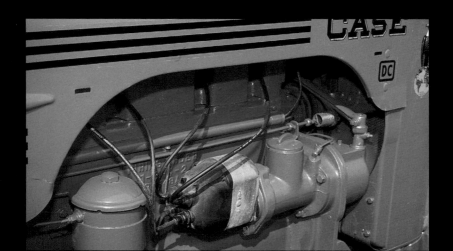

1949 Case DC

The D-series was powered by a 259-cubic-inch overhead-valve Case-built four-cylinder engine, versions of which could run on either gasoline or distillate. On gasoline, it produced 35.5 horsepower at the pulley; on distillate, 33.5. Some versions came with a three-speed transmission offering a top speed of about 5 mph; others had a four-speed allowing a top speed of 11 mph.

While Case offered electric starting and lights, the DC retained magneto ignition, allowing the owner to "remain independent of battery for ignition." In other words, should the battery go dead, the engine could be started more easily with the hand crank.

1949
John Deere R

Diesel engines began appearing in tractors in the early 1930s, their primary advantage being lower operating costs. But there were plenty of disadvantages as well. Higher initial cost was one; starting the engine on a cold morning was another.

Some manufacturers attempted to solve the latter problem by incorporating a compression release along with a gasoline fuel and ignition system: The operator would start the engine on gas, and once it was

warm, deactivate the compression release and switch to diesel. Another solution was to use a small gasoline engine as a starter motor, its exhaust warming the diesel engine and fuel before attempting to turn it over. Called a "pony engine," this was the method chosen by Deere when it introduced the Model R diesel tractor in 1949. Its 415-cubic-inch engine was rated at 45 drawbar horsepower, 51 at the pulley, making it the most powerful tractor in the John Deere lineup.

The Model R had a short life by company standards: It lasted only through 1954. But its styling would influence a future generation of Deeres, and its diesel engine would form the basis for many more to come.

Meet the new MODEL **R** **DIESEL**

'bringing you'

- The greater power and fuel economy of a diesel tractor.
- Exclusive two-cylinder simplicity that sets new standards in performance, maintenance costs, and years of service among wheel-type diesel tractors.
- Modern design with all the advantages of hydraulic Powr-Trol, live power take-off, electric starting and lighting equipment, and many others.

YOU'VE heard about this great new tractor. Many of you have seen it on trial runs throughout the country where it passed every test with flying colors. *Now, it's in production, and what a tractor it is!*

It's POWERFUL

A "heavyweight" among wheel types, the Model "R" has the knockout punch to whip those big jobs in a hurry—the stamina to slug it out continuously under heavy loads in hard, grueling conditions with fewer time-outs for adjustment and repair.

It's ECONOMICAL

Naturally, you expect greater fuel economy from a Diesel-type engine but you'll be surprised how

much farth "R." Its hi Equally im to be less b tractor—wi etc., requir engines. Th trouble . . .

It's RI

The same nated many it possible stronger—y dependable

...It's the COM

John Deere's first diesel, the Model R, was based on its gas-powered Model D. Both used a flat-twin engine, a familiar Deere feature. In this brochure, an R is shown pulling a five-bottom plow; the D was rated for three or four plows.

dollar goes in the Model engine is a "miser" on fuel. ntenance expense is bound odel "R" is a *two-cylinder* pistons, bearings, injectors, wheel-type Diesel tractor wear, greater freedom from repair bills.

BUILT

r simplicity that has elimi-Model "R" also has made ining parts larger, heavier, John Deere Diesel a more tractor.

It's MODERN

In modern design, the "R" is a standout: It has the famous John Deere Hydraulic Powr-Trol for effortless operation of heavy implements. Both Powr-Trol and the power shaft are controlled by an *independent clutch for continuous operation* when desired. There's a speed for every job. An auxiliary engine provides instant starting.

Comfortable seat . . . roomy, step-up platform : . . unobstructed view . . . convenient controls . . . foot-operated differential brakes . . . balanced weight with a highly-efficient steering mechanism—all contribute to an extreme ease of handling that's comparable to smaller tractors.

It's FIELD-PROVED

From drawing board to final production, the new Model "R" represents 12 years of designing, developing, and testing under the most severe conditions. It's a tractor you can buy with confidence, own with growing satisfaction through the years ahead.

From every angle, the Model "R" is the new leader in its field. Here at last is a really simple, easy-to-understand Diesel tractor that will provide the complete answer to your big power needs. Make arrangements with your John Deere dealer to see it at your earliest opportunity.

TE ANSWER to your BIG POWER NEEDS

1949
Massey-Harris 55 GS

When Massey-Harris introduced styled tractors in 1938, louvered engine covers contributed to their sleek looks. Unfortunately they also contributed to overheating problems, so the engine side panels were trimmed back and later removed altogether.

Like those of most other manufacturers, postwar Massey-Harris tractors typically came standard with pneumatic rubber tires; by this time, costs had come down considerably, and the advantages over steel-lugged wheels were too great to ignore. In fact, about the only point in favor of steel wheels was that they couldn't go flat.

When introduced in 1947, the Massey-Harris 55 became the biggest tractor in the company's lineup. While smaller M-H tractors still used flathead engines made by Continental, the larger models—

1949 Massey-Harris 55 GS

both gas and diesel—were fitted with overhead-valve engines built by M-H. Powering the 55 was a 382-cubic-inch four-cylinder gas engine providing 56 horsepower at the pulley.

1949
Oliver 70

Since the mid Thirties, Oliver tractors had been known for the sleek styling and smooth-running six-cylinder engines of the top models. Among them was the "70," which first appeared in 1935 with a 201-cubic-inch overhead-valve six rated at 27 horsepower. A revised 1940 version was boosted to 30 horsepower.

In terms of styling, these tractors were far ahead of their time. Though they carried the same

1949 Oliver 70

green-and-yellow color scheme as contemporary John Deeres, there was no mistaking the two—even it it weren't for the Oliver's red wheels. Though this example carries abbreviated rear fenders, some had full-coverage fenders sporting a graceful "ducktail" kick-up at the rear.

Oliver introduced its first diesel-powered tractor in 1940. A Buda-Lanova diesel engine was fitted to the 80, one of Oliver's unstyled models. The 80 could also be ordered with gasoline and distillate engines through the end of its production run in 1948. Shortly thereafter, Oliver's 60, 70, and 80 series tractors were all replaced by restyled models labeled 66, 77, and 88.

239

1950
International Harvester
Farmall Cub

As far as owners of small farms were concerned, few tools were as valuable or as versatile as the IH Farmall Cub. It was the smallest tractor in the Farmall line, designed for use on farms of less than 40 acres. Fitted with a small 60-cubic-inch flathead four-cylinder engine rated at about 9 horsepower, the Cub could pull one 12-inch plow. A three-speed transmission accompanied a foot-operated clutch.

A reversible, height-adjustable drawbar and universal mounting (all attaching parts remained on the tractor) eased

installation of plows, cultivators, and planters. Depending on attachments, the Cub could cover three to 15 acres a day. IH sales literature stressed the Cub's maneuverability and toughness, and noted that the tractor was an ideal auxiliary machine in large-farm situations where use of a full-size tractor was impossible or inefficient.

243

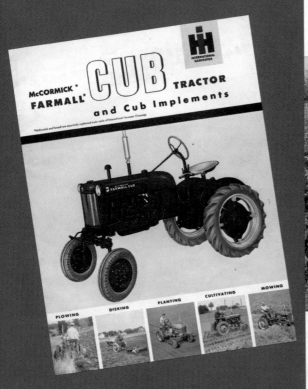

FARMALL CUB

Even in the early Fifties, many small farms still used horses in the fields. International's Cub was targeted at farmers working less than 40 acres, and its brochure depicted the little tractor performing a variety of chores.

You're farming 40 acres or less and you're tired of plodding behind horses, mules or a garden tractor . . . you're eager to do more work in less time . . . to handle more acres or have more leisure . . . to earn money with less physical effort. You want a small tractor to fit your needs and pocketbook.

International Harvester has provided the answer to your problem. The Farmall Cub and its implements are designed to provide a completely adequate working unit for the small-acreage farmer . . . part-time farmer . . . commercial truck grower . . . and a handy utility working unit or *extra* tractor for the large-acreage farmer.

To thousands of farmers who have never used tractor power before, the Farmall Cub has introduced a new system of farming—the Farmall System—which is at once faster, easier, better and more profitable. Every day hundreds of new users are learning that the Farmall Cub is a practical, easy-riding, power-plus tractor that does the work of two or three horses, mules or small garden tractors. With its "big tractor" features—high compression 4-cylinder engine, power take-off, and a complete line of sturdy

for small acreages...part-time farming...
vegetable growing...and large-farm utility

and low-cost *quick-change* implements—the Farmall Cub fills the need for a fullfledged but low-cost farm power unit.

Large-acreage farmers, too, have adopted the Cub as a handy tractor to have around. On Cub-sized belt, field or road jobs, it's cheaper to operate than larger tractors. It saves time and crops, too, by keeping the big tractor busy in the field. The Cub is especially handy for hauling jobs—on the farm, in the yard or on the road.

The Farmall Cub handles every two-horse or mule job—and *then some*. It outworks a team on all jobs, and handles some jobs two or three times as fast. It doesn't "eat" when it isn't working, and adds from 3 to 5 crop acres for each animal it replaces. And, besides, it is always ready and "harnessed for work!"

Fuel consumption on the many Cub jobs averages slightly over 2 quarts per hour. In a 10-hour day under average conditions you can plow 3½ acres, disk harrow 10 acres, field cultivate 15 acres, plant from 8 to 10 acres of corn or cotton, cultivate up to 12 acres, and mow from 12 to 15 acres.

The pictures on this page illustrate just a few of the many jobs the Farmall Cub handles with ease.

Grinding ear corn with a hammer mill and a Farmall Cub

Hauling corn with a Farmall Cub

inches deep with the Farmall Cub

Planting four rows of peas

Farmall Cub cultivating strawberries

Cutting alfalfa at a rate of 12 to 15 acres a day

1950
John Deere MT

Like its Model L and LA predecessors, the Model M of 1947 departed from usual John Deere practice in having its two-cylinder engine standing upright, mounted longitudinally in the frame; all other Deeres since the company's beginning had their engines laid flat with cylinders facing forward. The M also used the engine as a structural member, making it a "unit design."

Several new features marked the Model M. The padded seat included inflatable cushions and was

adjustable fore and aft, while the steering wheel could be telescoped through a one-foot range, allowing the driver to either stand or sit.

Originally introduced with a standard front end, the Model MT (for Tricycle) was added in 1949; two-wheeled tricycle and wide front ends appeared at the same time. MTs also boasted dual hydraulics, which allowed separate lift controls for the left and right side. And a new system of attaching implements greatly decreased the amount of time it took to connect and disconnect them.

A 101-cubic-inch engine delivered about 14 drawbar horsepower and just under 20 at the belt pulley. Though the one-plow-rated tractor was well-suited to smaller farms, it remained in the line only until 1952.

Ford tractors built after the company reentered the market in 1939 were distributed through Harry Ferguson, Inc., per an agreement that allowed Ford to include Ferguson's ingenious three-point hitch as standard equipment. Both the 9N (which took its name from its 1939 introduction) and its successor the 2N (which, likewise, indicated its 1942 debut) wore "Ferguson System" badges below the blue ovals on their grilles.

However, Ford and Ferguson went through a messy "divorce" after the war that included lawsuits on both sides, and their partnership was dissolved in July 1947. After that, Ford tractors still carried a three-point hitch, but Ferguson was no longer involved in distribution—nor was his name emblazoned on the grille.

Tractors produced after that time featured a number of changes, including a four-speed transmission to replace the former three-speed, and a new name again indicating its date of arrival: 8N. (Though technically they were introduced in mid 1947, Ford perhaps viewed them as 1948 models.)

Though the standard engine remained a 120-cubic-inch flathead four, conversions were available

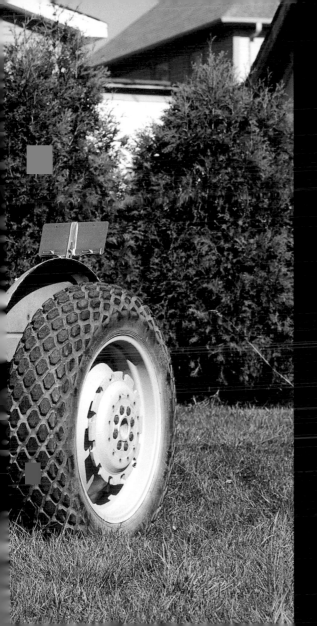

from several manufacturers to
adapt Ford's automotive engines
to its tractors in order to gain
more pulling power. Early conver-

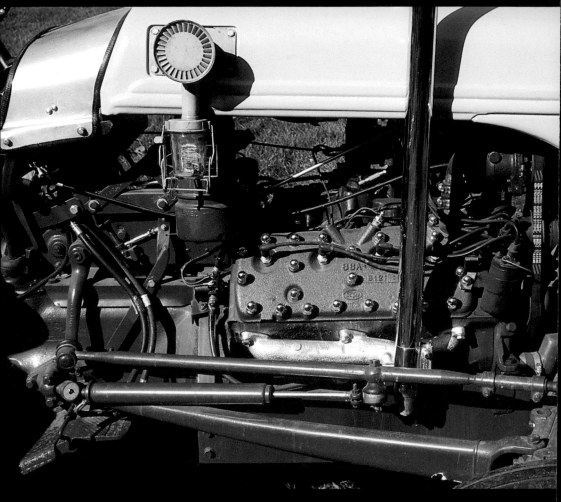

sions transplanted a 226-cubic-inch flathead six, but later ones provided even more power.

Our featured 8N has been fitted with a 255-cubic-inch Ford flathead V-8 truck engine courtesy of a Delbert conversion. Like the six-cylinder swaps, an engine-to-transmission adapter plate included mounting points for a separate frame that supported the front suspension, which in stock form was bolted directly to the engine.

1952
Ford 8N/Funk 6 & V-8

A mong those companies offering engine conversion kits for Ford tractors was Funk Brothers Aircraft. Odd name for a maker of hot-rod tractor kits? Not really. Funk Brothers started out building kit planes powered by Ford Model A engines. When the company heard about Oliver Glover's conversion for mounting a Ford flathead six into Ford tractors (*see* 1945 Ford 2N), it sent representatives to see if Funk Bros. could cast the engine-to-transmission adapter plate that Glover was welding

together out of several pieces of metal. Funk got the job and began making the plate and other necessary parts.

Eventually, Funk Bros. began selling its own kits for both six-cylinder and flathead V-8 conversions. One of each is represented here; a six-cylinder version is shown on the first four pages, a V-8 on the last four. In both cases, they differed from some other conversions in that the engines were fitted with special cast-iron oil pans that allowed the front suspension to be bolted directly to the pans, just as they were in the stock four-cylinder tractor. Other conversion kits used separate subframes to mount the front ends, because the automotive engines used stamped-steel pans that weren't strong enough.

In their day, these V-8 conversions were among the most powerful tractors available. But the mainline manufacturers—including Ford itself—eventually offered larger machines with stronger engines, and the popularity of conversion kits waned.

263

1953
Ford Jubilee

I n recognition of its
50th anniversary,
Ford introduced the
"Golden Jubilee" model
in 1953. The celebration
lasted longer than
expected, however, as
the Jubilee was built
through 1954. Larger,
sleeker, and more mod-
ern than the 8N that
preceded it, the Jubilee

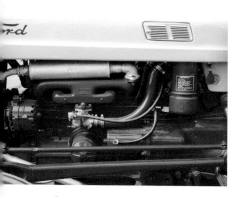

1953 Ford Jubilee

also introduced Ford's Red Tiger overhead-valve four-cylinder engine to replace the aging flathead four that had been in use since 1938. Displacing 134 cubic inches, it provided 25 horsepower at the drawbar, 31 at the pulley—an increase of more than 20 percent over the former 120-cubic-inch flathead. Also new was an optional "live" power take-off, which turned even when the tractor wasn't moving.

The Jubilee was replaced in 1955 with a new series of tractors that looked similar, but offered a variety of engines including Ford's first to run on LP Gas. A six-cylinder diesel followed in 1961. Though better known for its cars and trucks, Ford remains a big name in tractors to this day.

267

1954
Allis-Chalmers WD 45

Following the WC in 1948 was Allis-Chalmers' WD series. Though it carried the same 201-cubic-inch overhead-valve four-cylinder engine, that engine could now run on "tractor fuel," a cheaper, lower-grade alternative to gasoline. The WD proved very popular, selling more than 131,000 units during its six-year production span.

A longer stroke resulted in increased displacement (226 cubic inches) on the WD 45, introduced in 1953. Horsepower rose to 40 on gaso-

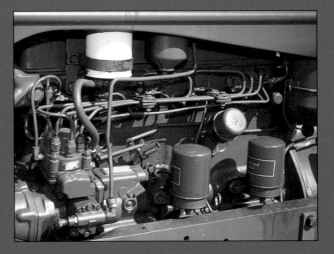

line, 32 on tractor fuel, and a new diesel version was also added. Built through 1957, the 45 proved nearly as popular as its predecessor, selling more than 83,000 units during its five-year run.

WD 45 Diesel models, like the tractor shown, carried a 230-cubic-inch engine rated at 43 horsepower. This example sports power-adjustable rear wheels, which allowed the track to be widened or narrowed to accommodate different row widths. The operator would loosen four wheel bolts on each side, and the track would gradually widen when the tractor was inched forward, and narrow when it was driven in reverse. WD 45s could be ordered with a choice of three front ends: single wheel; dual-wheel tricycle; and adjustable wide track, as shown here.

1954 Allis-Chalmers WO 45

1954
Case 500

In 1953, Case began a changeover in its model line that not only brought new mechanicals, but also new designations.

First to appear was the 500 series, which carried the first diesel engine offered by Case. This was a 377-cubic-inch six-cylinder rated at 64 horsepower at the pulley. Electric starting was standard (unusual, since many competing diesels of the period used gasoline "pony" engines for starting), as was electric lighting and dual disc brakes. Another Case "first" for the 500 was power steering, helpful on a tractor that weighed a hefty 8100 pounds. A four-speed transmission gave a 10-mph top speed.

The 500 was quickly followed by smaller 300- and 400-series tractors, and in 1957 Case added 600-, 700-, 800-, and 900-series models

1954 Case 500

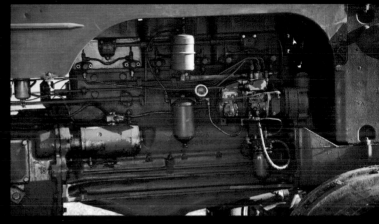

to the line. Also in 1957, the company broke into the crawler market with the acquisition of American Tractor Company, makers of the Terratrac.

In 1967, Case was purchased by the Kern County Land Company, then sold to Tenneco. It was during this time that "Old Abe," Case's eagle mascot that dated back to the time of the Civil War, was retired. In 1972, Case purchased English manufacturer David Brown Tractors, a company linked to Harry Ferguson and his famous three-point hitch.

Today, Case is allied with International Harvester, which Tenneco purchased during the economic recession of the early Eighties. Case-IH, whose parent companies date back to the 1860s and early 1900s, respectively, remains a prominent force in the agricultural field.

1954
International Harvester Farmall Super M-TA

The beauty of IH's Torque Amplifier (the "TA" in "M-TA") was that it allowed operators to instantly boost pulling power by as much as 45 percent, in any gear, without clutching or changing gears. The feature was especially useful in hard soil, soft or wet soil, and on upward grades. Turns at ends of rows became quicker because the operator could slow the machine without slipping the clutch or throttling back on the engine, which invited stalls. A simple back-

ward pull on the TA control lever engaged the torque amplifier; a shove forward and the tractor was instantly restored to the previous gear speed and power. The setup was separate from IH's standard five-speed shift pattern, so engagement and disengagement could be learned almost instantly. TA provided ten forward speeds, two in reverse. In 1954, no other tractor system allowed as wide a range of travel speeds.

Standard Super M-TA tractors ran on gasoline or distillate and were rated for three

1954 International Harvester Farmall Super M-TA

plows. Each diesel model, like the tractor seen here, was designated "Super M-TA Diesel." A grille design that was new for 1954 had side-located eye-bolts to accommodate support rods of front-mounted equipment.

McCORMICK
FARMALL

285

1954
Massey-Harris 44

The Massey-Harris postwar lineup started with the little 12-horsepower Pony and extended to the big 55 gas and diesel models. The Pony used a small Continental four-cylinder flathead engine, the 55s an M-H-built overhead-valve four. In between were the 22, 30, and 44, their numeric designations approximating horsepower output, though most tested higher.

Three engines were offered in the 44: an M-H four-cylinder in both gas and diesel versions, and also a Continental six. The 44 pictured is equipped with the M-H gas four. This 44 was one of the last tractors to carry the Massey-Harris name. That's not to say, however, that the company folded.

1954 Massey-Harris 44

Harry Ferguson, who held the patent for the famous three-point hitch, had long been allied with Ford. After the war, however, there was a parting of the ways, and Harry Ferguson, Inc. found itself in need of funds. In 1953, Ferguson merged with Massey-Harris to form Massey-Harris-Ferguson, which soon became simply Massey-Ferguson—as it remains to this day.

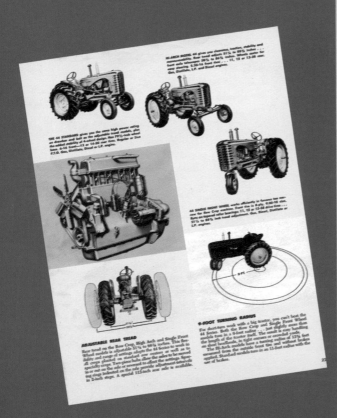

Versatility and maneuverability are stressed in the Massey-Harris brochure for the 44. Also shown is a cutaway view highlighting its mechanical features.

maintains volt bat- assures engine and lights

One-piece intake and exhaust manifold is machined for perfect fit. Specially designed metal-backed gasket eliminates dust and dirt. Intake passages deliver equal amount of fuel to each cylinder.

Valve-in-head engine provides easier starting, more power. Ball and socket connection between rocker arm and valve stem reduces wear. Exhaust valves rotate.

Sleeves are precision cast and machined for accurate fit, easy replacement. Positively sealed. Pistons have four rings—three compression, one oil control—for a tight seal, full compression.

Sealed water pump—grease packed—directs water through gallery to valves and head. Pump has double bearings—runs smooth, requires less power. Thermostat has large-capacity by-pass. Holds 22 U.S. quarts.

The built-in centrifugal governor is quickly responsive to load requirements. Linked to the dual-float carburetor, it suits fuel consumption to the job. Adjusts from outside. Pressure lubricated.

MASSEY-HARRIS

Worm and sector steering gear reduces field and road shocks . . . eliminates backlash. Front wheel is set behind the vertical column for easier steering.

Cast front and rear wheels are standard on all models to give added weight. The Row Crop front wheels are reversible to give added clearance.

The heavy-duty, 11-inch clutch on the 44 Special assures positive plate and face contact, full engine power to the transmission. Nine pressure springs equalize contact.

Full-pressure lubrication results in positive protection for bearings, shafts and pistons. Pump delivers measured quantities—circulates proper amount for correct oiling.

Block and upper crankcase are cast in one piece. Crankshaft is perfectly balanced while in motion and at rest to assure a smooth power stroke.

1954
Minneapolis-Moline G

In 1941, Minneapolis-Moline became the first manufacturer to offer production tractors that ran on LP Gas (Liquefied Propane Gas), which offered better fuel economy and reduced maintenance compared to gasoline. Other manufacturers soon joined in, but both LPG and gasoline engines were soon overshadowed by the efficiencies of the diesel.

1954 Minneapolis-Moline G

Rudolph Diesel invented the engine that bears his name back in 1892, but they didn't find use in tractors until the early 1930s. And they didn't find use at M-M until 20 years after that.

In fact, it was 1953 before M-M offered diesels. They were available in a variety of models, one being the Model G, which had been introduced in 1940 as M-M's stoutest tractor of the period. It carried a 426-cubic-inch six-cylinder diesel rated at 63 horsepower at the pulley. The G was a hefty brute that in diesel form tipped the scales at 8200 pounds.

In 1963, Minneapolis-Moline was purchased by White Motor Corporation, and by the end of the decade had been merged with Oliver and Cockshutt (a Canadian firm) to form White Farm Equipment Company.

1958
John Deere 820

I n the early 1950s, John Deere began renaming its tractors, with numeric designations replacing the letters used since the company's inception. First among these were the 50 and 60 in 1952 (replacing the B and A, respectively), followed by the 70 gas and diesel (G), 40 (M), and finally the diesel 80 (replacing the R) in 1955. One significant milestone of this period was Deere's introduction of power steering in 1954. Another was

1958 John Deere 820

the adoption of a "live" PTO, already used on competitor's machines, which allowed the PTO to turn whether or not the tractor was moving. Also newly available were engines powered by Liquefied Propane Gas (LP Gas).

Two digits gave way to three in 1956, all designations ending in "20." Many improvements marked the change, among them the adaptation of Deere's version of Ferguson and Ford's revolutionary three-point hitch. Most notable, visually, were the bold yellow side stripes and sun-reflective yellow seat.

Models ranged from the little 320, with around 25 horsepower, to the big 820 with nearly 73 horsepower. The latter used a tiny 19-cubic-inch V-4 gas "pony engine" to start the 472-cubic-inch diesel, which maintained Deere's traditional horizontal twin-cylinder layout.

299

1959
Oliver 660

Replacing the 66, 77, and 88 models in 1954 was the "Super" series (Super 66, etc.). It was in this series that several new features were introduced to the Oliver line, including independent PTO, independent disc brakes, Hydra-Lectric hydraulic system, and a three-point hitch. New to the line was the Super 99, a version of which was powered by a General Motors three-cylinder two-stroke diesel. The Super series looked to be a step backward in the styling department, abandoning the sleek lines and enclosed hoods of previous models for a squarer, upright design with an open-sided engine compartment.

This "new" look continued when the Super series was replaced by the 550, 660, 770,

1959 Oliver 660

and 880 models in the late 1950s. Styling was revised only slightly, but colors changed from dark green and yellow to medium green and white.

Our featured 660 is powered by a 155-cubic-inch four-cylinder engine which, despite its small size, gave the 3200-pound tractor a three-plow rating. The 660 was built from 1959 to 1964.

In 1960, Oliver became a subsidiary of White Motor Corporation. White then purchased Cockshutt (a Canadian tractor builder) in 1962, and Minneapolis-

1959 Oliver 660

Moline a year later.
In 1969, the three
tractor manufactur-
ers were combined
to form the White
Farm Equipment
Company. After-
ward, some tractors
that were identical
except for paint and
trim were sold
under the
Minneapolis-
Moline, Oliver, and
White names.
Starting in the mid
Seventies, all were
simply badged
"White."

1960
John Deere 630

T he paint was barely dry on its 20-series tractors
when John Deere introduced the 30 series in
1958. But the differences were largely cosmetic. The
sides of the hood were given an angular bottom cut
and painted solid yellow, while the numeric designation was moved up even with the "JOHN DEERE"
lettering. Gauges and controls were modified, some

models gaining an automotive-style layout, and seats were made more comfortable. Higher-level models received new rear fenders incorporating then-trendy quad headlights. At the rear, controls for the dual hydraulic system were cleaned up.

The same models returned, starting with the 330 and running through the 730, with the 830 arriving in 1959. Our featured 630 is powered by a 303-cubic-inch engine rated at about 44 horsepower and is fitted with an adjustable front track.

It would turn out to be the final year for the horizontal twin-cylinder engine that had been a company tradition since 1923. Thereafter came four- and six-cylinder models that would herald the modern era at John Deere.

As tractors grew increasingly more sophisticated in the 1960s, manufacturers looked to their engineering departments to provide them with a leg up on competitors. When International Harvester introduced the 504 Tractor in 1962, the company emphasized its "New Super-Sensitive 3-point draft controlled hitch"— which gave automatic control of implements in all types of soil and terrain. Whether the operator wanted uniform depth of imple-

ments or depth that would change to follow soil contours, the draft-controlled hitch could do it. All of this was controlled by just two levers: one to raise or lower the implement into position, the other to set working depth and draft load.

The 504 was offered with gasoline, LP Gas, and diesel engines. Our featured example carries a 152-cubic-inch engine that delivered 46 horsepower at the PTO on gasoline. With International's Torque Amplifier system providing ten forward speeds, the 504 could travel at up to 17 mph. Its Dyna-Life clutch had a claimed life five times greater than that of a fiber clutch.

International Harvester, which had long been the most prominent name in tractors, surrendered that title to John Deere in the late Seventies. An economic recession in the early Eighties prompted several business changes, including the sale of International's construction-equipment division. In 1984, IH was purchased by Tenneco, which already owned Case, and the two manufacturers were eventually combined to form Case-International, as its tractors are known today.

Scale Models

Farmall 460 by ERTL 1/16 scale

While collecting classic tractors can be fun and rewarding, the hobby can consume large amounts of money and space—just ask some of the owners. But collecting *model* tractors demands far less of both. Following is just a sample of the wide selection of models available. Model manufacturers are noted in the caption of each photo; their phone numbers and web addresses (where available) are listed at right. Other good sources include hobby shops and tractor dealers.

Danbury Mint   203-853-2000
www.danburymint.com

ERTL
www.racingchampions.com

Franklin Mint   (800) 843-6468
www.franklinmint.com

Spec Cast
www.speccast.com

Allis-Chalmers D-17 by ERTL 1/16 scale

Scale Models

Case Steam Tractor by ERTL 1/16 scale

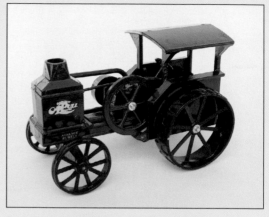

Rumely OilPull by Scale Models 1/16 scale

John Deere Model D by ERTL 1/16 scale

Massey-Harris 4WD by Scale Models 1/16 scale

Fordson by Danbury Mint 1/16 scale

Ford 8N by Danbury Mint 1/16 scale

Oliver OC-3 by ERTL 1/16 scale

John Deere 40 Crawler by ERTL 1/16 scale

Scale Models

John Deere 720 by ERTL 1/16 scale

Oliver Standard 88 by Spec Cast 1/16 scale

Minneapolis-Moline UDLX by Scale Models 1/16 scale

Farmall H by ERTL 1/16 scale

John Deere Model A by ERTL 1/16 scale

John Deere Model B by ERTL 1/16 scale

Farmall Super C by ERTL 1/16 scale

Ford Jubilee by Franklin Mint 1/12 scale